MUSLIM JURISPRUDENCE AND THE QURANIC LAW OF CRIMES

MIR WALI ULLAH

Peace Publications
42-Manzoor Manzal Urdu-Bazar Lahore

2023
Publish by:
Syed Zulfiqar Jaffri
Peace Publications Lahore

Printed by:
Haji Hanif Printer Lahore, Pakistan

Binder: Qayyum Ahmad

ISBN:969-9988-29-5
ISBN:978-969-9988-29-5

Peace Publications
42.Manzoor Manzal Opp Govt Muslim
Model High School Urdu Bazar Lahore
E-mail:peace_publications@yahoo.com
Ph:042-37361448 Cell:0322-4298311

MUSLIM JURISPRUDENCE
AND THE
QURANIC LAW OF CRIMES

PUBLISHERS' NOTE

The first edition of this book by late Mir Wali Ullah (formerly Principal, Law College, Peshawar University) was published by the author some years ago (no date of publication is given) from Abbottabad under the title *The Quranic Law of Crimes and Lectures on Muslim Jurisprudence.* "The Quranic Law of Crimes" covered only the first twenty-six pages, while the rest of the book, pages 27-151, related to "Muslim Jurisprudence".

For this, the second edition, the original arrangement has been reversed, placing the part relating to Muslim Jurisprudence first. The part relating to the Quranic Law of Crimes comes second.

Authors are not usually good editors and proof-readers. Mir Wali Ullah was a solid scholar, but he does not seem to be aware of the methodology of book-making. He has given substantial food for thought, but he did not make a scientific presentation.

We are grateful to Mr M. Ashraf Darr (Hon. Secretary and Publication Adviser to the Institute of Islamic Culture, Lahore) for his suggestions in the reshaping of the book. Int his edition, the names of persons, titles of books and technical terms have been properly transliterated, Quranic verses checked and corrected.

The book in its present shape, it is hoped, will be of great help and use to the law student and the general reader.

CONTENTS

آہ ! محکومی و تقلید و زوال تحقیق
خود بدلتے نہیں، قرآں کو بدل دیتے ہیں

—اقبال (''ضرب کلیم'')

Part One

MUSLIM JURISPRUDENCE

Chapter 1

THE SOURCES OF MUSLIM LAW

The question "What are the sources of Muslim Law ?" has been answered by almost all the Muslim jurists in these words: "There are four sources of Muslim Law: (1) the *Kitāb*, i.e. the Qur'ān; (2) the *Sunnah* or the *Sunnat*, i.e. the *Ḥadīth* (traditions); (3) the *Ijmā'*, i.e. the consensus, and (4) the *Qiyās*, i.e. analogical deductions."

Both the question and the answer seem to be simple enough, but, as we will see, they are not so simple as they seem to be.

List Neither Exhaustive Nor Logical. In the first place, the list is not exhaustive in any sense. Definitely and undeniably, there are other sources of Muslim Law as well, mention of which has purposely been omitted due to certain false prejudices. We will see later what those sources are. Secondly, the division is not logical inasmuch as it is not free from overlapping and the list is not strictly in the order of merit which it claims.

As a matter of fact, the prejudices referred to above have been so strong that some of the more orthodox writers would rather curtail the above list than agree to enlarge it. For example, Maulānā 'Abdullah b. Aḥmad b. Maḥmūd Abul-Barakāt Nasafī (d. 710/1310) mentions even *Qiyās* as the fourth source of Muslim Law very reluctantly. His reluctance is apparent from the following statement with which his well-known text-book on Muslim jurisprudence, the *Al-Manār*, begins : "The sources of Muslim Law are three : (1) the *Kitāb*, (2) the *Sunnat*, (3) the *Ijmā' al-Ummat* and the fourth source is *Qiyās*." And it should be remembered that Nasafī is the author of the *Kanz al-Daqā'iq*, one of the most popular text-books on Muslim Law.

Likewise, Shāh Walīullah Muḥaddith Dihlawī (d. 1176/1762) in his *Al-Balāgh al-Mubīn* says : "There are three *uṣūl* for all Islamic affairs : (1) the *āyāt-i muḥkam* of the Qur'ān, (2) the *Aḥādīth-i ṣaḥīḥah* and (3) the *ijmā'-i ṣaḥābah*."

As we will see later, some of our more inflexible jurists have gone so far as to omit even the *ijmā'* from the list. According to them the *Kitāb* and the *Sunnah* are the only two sources of law. They maintain that God and His Prophet have given us rules of law for all conceivable contingencies that might possibly arise anywhere and at any time. They are not prepared to believe that these two sources of law had not provided legislation for any peculiar or particular combination of facts and circumstances, which a law case could ever be made of.

It would not be out of place here to make a passing mention of a hostile minority amongst the Muslims who would not recognise even the *Sunnah* as a source of Muslim Law. In their opinion, it is only the ordinances of the Qur'ān that have the binding force and can control, hold in check and direct the acts of legislation by the Muslims.

On the other hand, some of the modern writers on Muslim Law and jurisprudence, both Muslims and non-Muslims, have added "custom" as the fifth source of our laws. They have briefly referred to some other sources as well, but have not cared to add them to the list. However, the majority of the modern writers, as well, stick to the time-honoured old list of four.

A number of Muslim writers of old, some of whom were eminent lawyers and jurists, suggested other sources of Muslim Law such as *Istiḥsān*, *Ta'āmul* and *Istiṣlāḥ*, etc., but they were not generally accepted and could not, therefore, be included in the list.

I will try, in this chapter, to present a complete list of these sources as far as I have been able to determine them in the limited scope of my studies of the subject. I know, much of difference of opinion is possible, rather probable, on what I would say, but I am, as well, sure that the reader would agree with me when I say that an honest and well-intentioned difference of opinion has always been a healthy sign of life during the progressive stages of all branches of learning.

Now, taking the list as it is, we will deal with the four sources of Muslim Law, one by one.

(1) *Qur'ān*. The first on the list and naturally the first in authority is the *Kitāb*, i.e. the Qur'ān. We believe that the Book is the word of God and we further believe that it is His last word. It follows, therefore, that the laws given by the Qur'ān are eternal, immutable and binding on Muslims of all countries and of all ages. The only honest way out for those unfortunate Muslims who think that these laws have lived out their life and are out of date today is to get out of the fold of Islam. Unfortunatel,y such people do exist at the time.

As a matter of fact, the Qur'ān has given us a few laws and some general principles of law and left the bulk of social, political, constitutional and international laws open for the Muslims to legislate for themselves in different countries and different ages, in the light of their existing conditions and circumstances. Out of six thousand six hundred and sixty-six verses of the Holy Book, only about five hundred verses relate to matters of law, both secular and ecclesiastical. A careful study of the Book would show beyond the shadow of doubt that there is not a word in it which could ever become time-barred.

Throughout the history of Muslim Law, the Muslim jurists and lawyers have upheld the finality of the principles and rules of law framed by the Qur'ān. There has never been any difference of opinion on the proposition that the *muḥkamāt* of the Book, i.e. the ordinances of the Qur'ān given in plain, perspicuous and unambiguous words, are the final authority on a point of law covered by them. But, unfortunately, a great deal of divergence of opinion exists on almost each and every point of law given by the Quranic verses. This unhappy state of affairs is due to the different interpretations put on these verses.

Naskh. The first and the foremost of the causes of difference of opinion in this respect is the question of *naskh*, i.e. the repeal and abrogation of one verse of the Qur'ān by another. This question arises from the following verse of the Holy Book itself:

ما ننسخ من اية او ننسها نات بخير منها او مثلها

[“Whatever message (verse) We abrogate or cause to be forgotten, We bring one better than it or one like it” (ii. 106).]

Now, the question is whether the *naskh* mentioned in this verse relates to the abrogation of one verse of the Qur'ān by another verse or it relates to the repeal of certain laws given in the old revealed books by the laws promulgated by the Qur'ān. A reference to the context would clearly show that the *naskh* in this verse refers to the abrogation of the old laws by the new ones given in the Qur'ān. The verse immediately preceding the verse under consideration runs as follows: "Neither those who disbelieve from among the people of the Book (the Jews and the Christians), nor the polytheists, like that any good (*khair*) should be sent down to you from your Lord" (ii. 105). We find that the word *khair* used in verse 105 refers to the verses of the Qur'ān as compared with the old books. It would be safer, therefore, to interpret the word *khair* in verse 106 as well in the same sense.

But it cannot be denied that a big majority of our lawyers and jurists have held that some verses of the Qur'ān stand repealed by some other verses of it. It may be noted here that there is no *ḥadīth* directly traceable to the Holy Prophet declaring that a certain verse in the Qur'ān has been abrogated. The question whether a particular verse is or is not *mansūkh* has always been the subject of individual opinion. Therefore, there have always been widely divergent views as to the number of Quranic verses that stand repealed. Most of our *mufassirīn*, the commentators of the Holy Book, have declared no less than five hundred of the Quranic verses as repealed. Just one verse of the Qur'ān, popularly known as the *āyah-i saif*, i.e. the verse of the sword, which for the first time declared *jihād* lawful for the Muslims is said to be responsible for the repeal of one hundred and twenty-four verses of the Qur'ān. Even "There is no compulsion in the matter of religion" (ii. 256) is said to have been abrogated by the *āyah-i saif.*

'Allāmah Jalāl al-Dīn Suyūṭī (d. 911/1505), one of the authors of the *Tafsīr-i Jalālain* and the author of the *Tafsīr-i Ittiqān*, etc., puts the number of repealed verses at twenty. Shāh Walīullah Muḥaddith Dihlawī (d. 1176/1762), the most renowned Muslim scholar of the twelfth/eighteenth century puts this number at five.

In this connection, a most pitiable situation has been created by a fairly large number of our jurists, who hold that a *ḥadīth* as well can repeal a verse of the Qur'ān. More than one instance of such a repeal can be found in books of Muslim Law. Some of them go still farther and say that a Quranic ordinance can be abrogated by the *Ijmā'* as well. An interesting instance of a repeal of this nature may be cited here with advantage. The *Ifādat al-Shuyūkh* by Maulānā Nawwāb Sayyid Muḥammad Ṣiddīq Ḥasan (d. 1308/1890) says : "According to some jurists, the Quranic verse :

وَمَنْ يَقْتُلْ مُؤْمِنًا مُتَعَمِّدًا فَجَزَاؤُهُ جَهَنَّمُ خَالِدًا فِيهَا

["And whoever kills a believer intentionally, his punishment is Hell abiding therein for ever" (iv. 93)] stands repealed by the *Ijmā'* in case the murderer is a Muslim."

This furnishes a glaring illustration of the sad attitude of some of our jurists who would be prepared to declare a Quranic verse repealed because it goes against their prejudices. The prejudice in this case is that a Muslim cannot be sent to Hell for all times, under any circumstances. This reminds one of the Jews :

وَقَالُوا لَن تَمَسَّنَا النَّارُ إِلَّا أَيَّامًا مَّعْدُودَةً

["And they say : Fire will not touch us but for a few days" (ii. 80).]

The question whether the word *Khālidā* used in iv. 93 above and many other verses of the Holy Book means mathematical or philosophical eternity or just a long time, is beyond the scope of this chapter.

The proposition that a Quranic verse could be abrogated by the *Sunnah* or the *Ijmā'* seems on the face of it nothing less than blasphemous. This question shall be gone into in greater detail later.

Those who believe in the repeal of a Quranic verse by another Quranic verse have furnished the following list of the different kinds of such repeal :

(1) The law given by the verse is repealed, but its words remain part of the Qur'ān. The words of the repealing verse form part of the Qur'ān as well.

(2) The law given by the verse is repealed and its words also no longer form part of the Qur'ān. The repealing verse exists in the Qur'ān.

(3) The law given by the verse is repealed, but its words remain part of the Qur'ān. The repealing verse no longer remains part of the Qur'ān though the law given by it is yet in force.

(4) The law given by the verse is repealed and its words also no longer form part of the Qur'ān. The law given by the repealing verse is still in force but its words are no longer part of the Qur'ān.

(5) The law given by the verse is still in force but its words no longer form part of the Qur'ān and the repealing verse is not known.

(6) The repealing verse is repealed and the words of the repealing and repealed verses no longer form part of the Qur'ān.

The framers of this list have, as well, given instances of all these kinds of repeal from the Qur'ān. A careful consideration of the list would show that it is simply fantastic and ridiculous.

But throughout the history of Muslim jurisprudence there has always existed a minority which has held that no verse of the Holy Book has ever been abrogated. Abū Muslim Iṣfahānī (d. 138/755) has said that the repeal of a Quranic verse, though possible in theory, has never occurred in practice. On the other hand, Qāḍī Muḥammad b. 'Alī Shaukānī (d. 1255/1839) says that if Abū Muslim said so, he was a *jāhil* and the difference of opinion of a *jāhil* matters little. The intolerance of this nature shown by the majority of our writers has had the deplorable effect of retarding the progress of Muslim thought to a great extent.

It may be noted here that Muslim writers, lawyers and jurists of the present century, Hijri era, have totally rejected the theory of the repeal of the Quranic verses in any way.

Shān-i Nuzūl. Another cause of the difference of opinion in connection with the interpretation of the verses of the Holy Book is the habit of many of our *Mufassirīn* to undertake to hunt out stories alleged to furnish occasions for the revelation of these verses. It cannot be denied that some of these *shān-i nuzūl* stories, just a small number of them, are true, but writers like Muḥammad b. Isḥāq Wāqidī and Kalbī have gone so far as to give a story of that nature for each and every one of the verses of the Book. The

Muhaddithīn have denied the truth of almost all such stories but, unfortunately, these fruitless efforts have succeeded in creating mischief to a considerable extent.

The mention of a story as the background of a verse cannot fail to affect its interpretation. In most cases it unduly limits the scope of the application of the verse which would otherwise be general.

It would suffice here to give one of the most scandalous instances of these *shān-i nuzūl* stories. This story is attached to the following Quranic verse:

وَمَآ أَرْسَلْنَا مِن قَبْلِكَ مِن رَّسُولٍ وَلَا نَبِيٍّ إِلَّآ إِذَا
تَمَنَّىٰٓ أَلْقَى ٱلشَّيْطَٰنُ فِىٓ أُمْنِيَّتِهِۦ فَيَنسَخُ ٱللَّهُ مَا يُلْقِى
ٱلشَّيْطَٰنُ ثُمَّ يُحْكِمُ ٱللَّهُ ءَايَٰتِهِۦ ۗ وَٱللَّهُ عَلِيمٌ حَكِيمٌ

["And We never sent a messenger or a prophet before thee but when he desired (or recited), the devil put something in his desire (or recitation); but Allah annuls that which the devil casts, then does Allah establish His signs (or messages). And Allah is Knowing, Wise" (xxii. 52).]

As appears from the translation of the verse, the word *tamannā* may mean either "desired" or "recited". Imām Fakhr al-Dīn Rāzī, in his great commentary the *Mafātīḥ al-Ghaib*, popularly known as the *Tafsīr-i Kabīr*, gives both these meanings to the word and bases his opinion on an Arabic couplet wherein the word is used for recitation. But this meaning is rarely given to the word. The usual meaning of the word is "desire". Now it is a very well-known principle of interpretation recognised by all our jurists that a word can be given its rare meaning only in case the usual meaning is not possible in the context. But several of our *Mufassirīn* have given this rare meaning to the word *tamannā* in this verse. According to them, the verse means that when a prophet recites verses of the revealed Book the devil sometimes adds something to the recitation. Having given this meaning to the verse under consideration, they have narrated the following story as its *shān-i nuzūl*: "One day the Prophet was reciting the Holy Qur'ān. When he read :

أَفَرَءَيْتُمُ اللّٰتَ وَالْعُزّٰى ۙ وَمَنٰوةَ الثَّالِثَةَ الْأُخْرٰى

the devil put the following words as well in his mouth :

تلك الغرانيق العلى و ان شفاعتهن لترتجى

Later the words put in by the devil were annulled." Now the whole thing taken together means: "Have you then considered Lāt and 'Uzzā and another, the third, Manāt? (liii. 19, 20). These are exalted female idols and their *shafā'at*, i.e. intercession, is to be sought."

The Lāt, the 'Uzzā and the Manāt were the three female idols worshipped by the *Jāhilī* Arabs. This most wicked story, which is much longer, is narrated by Ṭabarī, Wāqidī, Abū Ḥātim, Ibn Mundhir and several other *Muḥaddithīn*. Most of the Muslim scholars of all times have rejected the story and some of them have conclusively proved that it is a fabrication made by some *Zindīq* and, as we know, the *Zindīqs* have, in the garb of Muslims, done great harm to the cause of Islam. But careless writers being over-anxious to find out stories which could furnish the *shān-i nuzūl* of the Quranic verses accepted the story and cited it in their works. It is exceedingly surprising to find a man of the learning of Imām-i Rabbānī Mujaddid Alf-i Thānī, in one of his letters, believing in the truth of this silly story. The *riwāyāt* of this type, though loudly denounced, never fail to poison some minds at least.

Hair-splitting and Philosophy. Yet another source of trouble in this respect is the introduction of the philosophical methods of discussion and consequential hair-splitting in connection with the interpretation of the Quranic verses. During the time of the 'Abbāsī caliphs most of the works of Plato and Aristotle and other Greek philosophers and several books of Vedantic philosophy were translated into Arabic, whereupon the Muslim scholars took to the study of philosophy wholeheartedly, with the result that even the commentaries of the Holy Book became brimful with philosophical discussions and useless over-subtleties. One would hardly believe it if one were told that some of our *Mufassirīn* have gone so far in this respect as to discuss the question whether the *baqarah* of Banī Isrā'īl was an ox or a cow and whether the dog of *Aṣḥāb-i Kahf* was spotted white and black or was red. It was, therefore, that it was said about one of such commentaries on the Qur'ān that it contained everything except the commentary on the Qur'ān.

It is not possible to deny the most valuable service the 'Ajamī writers have done to the cause of the advancement of Islamic literature. Almost all the commentaries on the Holy Book were written by these scholars. Likewise the compilers of the *Ṣiḥāḥ Sittah*, the six most reliable and popular collections of *Ḥadīth*, were all 'Ajamīs. Most of the other *Muḥaddithīn*, as well, like Dārimī, Dāraquṭnī, Ḥākim, Baihāqī and Baghawī, and others were from 'Ajam. All the same it is a fact that the simplicity, unaffectedness and non-artificiality of the Islamic tenets were seriously and adversely affected by the writings of these scholars. The Qur'ān, as the Qur'ān itself repeatedly says, is an easily understandable book. But most of the commentaries written by the 'Ajamīs have, unfortunately, made the Holy Book a mess of bewildering complications. You read a verse of the Qur'ān and you are in a perfectly clear atmosphere. You read the commentary on it and you find yourself in thick mist where visibility is at its lowest ebb. These writers have wasted much of time, paper and ink on laboured and lengthy explanations of the *Mutashābihāt* of the Holy Book. I have with me a book of no less than six hundred pages solely devoted to the explanation of these words of the Qur'ān : ثم استوی علی العرش. It was this state of affairs which made Khāqānī (d. 595/1198) say:

فلسفه در سخن میامیزید　　وانگهاں نام آں جدل منهید
اسپ دیں را که زادهٔ عرب است　　داغ یونانش بر کفل منهید

The true position in this matter was never more beautifully stated than in the following words of the *Fauz al-Kabīr*: "We will wholeheartedly and with the greatest submissiveness and respect accept those meanings of the Quranic verses which may be understood from their plain Arabic as spoken and understood by the Arabs, but we shall never agree that any hidden meanings which could be discovered only by the deep ponderings of these philosophers could ever have been meant to be the import of the words of God."

Rules of Interpretation. Difference of opinion based on different interpretations put on a text is very natural and cannot be avoided. An honest and well-considered opinion must be tolerated even if it does not agree with the generally accepted view on a point. But opinions based on sectarian prejudices are a real and serious source of trouble, and, unfortunately, we are faced with innumerable differences of opinion on all sorts of law points, which are mainly the result of such prejudices. Our jurists have rendered very valuable services to the cause of Muslim legal literature and have, from time to time, made rich contributions to it. They have framed useful and exhaustive rules of interpretation of texts, covering all conceivable aspects of the question. The earliest attempt at the compilation of *Uṣūl-i Fiqh*, the Principles of Muslim Law or Muslim Jurisprudence, was the work of Imām Shāfi'ī. It was followed by many other books on the subject, written at different times. The more popular of these works are *Al-Manār* referred to above, its commentary *Nūr al-Anwār*, the *Uṣūl al-Shāshī* and the *Talwīḥ-o Tauḍīḥ.* But some of these books as well enter into intricate, unimportant and sometimes absolutely useless niceties and trivial minutia.

(2) *Ḥadīth.* And now we come to the second source of Muslim Law, the second on the list and second in authority. It is the *Sunnah*, i.e. the *Ḥadīth* coming down from the Prophet himself. The author of the *Nūr al-Anwār*, Ḥāfiẓ Shaikh Aḥmad, the tutor of Emperor 'Ālamgīr Aurangzeb, defines *Sunnah* and *Ḥadīth* in the following words: "*Sunnah* means the words, the acts and the acquiescence of the Prophet and the words and acts of his Companions, and *Ḥadīth*

means the words of the Prophet only." Technically, the definition is correct, but the words *Sunnah* and *Ḥadīth* are generally used as synonymous. According to the *Nūr al-Anwār*, there are about three thousand *aḥādīth* which actually refer to law points, both ritual and secular.

This part of our subject is both delicate and difficult. There are people who would like to make us believe that a *ḥadīth* is so powerful an authority that it may abrogate an ordinance promulgated by the Qur'ān itself. On the other extreme there are those who would say that *ḥadīth* is no authority on any point of law, at all. One has, therefore, to be very cautious in the discussion that follows.

Ḥadīth during Khilāfat-i Rāshidah. I think it would be useful to begin the discussion of this subject with a brief reference to the history of the publication of *Ḥadīth* traditions. The Prophet himself asked his followers not to write down anything he said except the Qur'ān and ordered them to destroy the *Ḥadīth* collections if they had made any. He destroyed some of these collections himself. It has been said that "the reason for this prohibition was that the Qur'ān was being revealed at the time and it was feared that if *aḥādīth* were reduced into writing, they would get mixed up with the Qur'ān. After the Prophet, when the Quranic verses got compiled in book form, this apprehension disappeared and the Muslims saw no objection to the *aḥādīth* being written down."

There is no reliable evidence that any *Ḥadīth* collection was prepared during the time of Abū Bakr. Imām Dhahabī (d. 748/1347), in his well-known biographical work, the *Tadhkirat al-Ḥuffāẓ*, has said:

" 'Ā'ishah says that her father (Abū Bakr) prepared a collection containing five hundred *aḥādīth*. One night he could not sleep and kept pondering over the matter. The next morning he burnt the collection to ashes and said that it was possible that he considered a *rāvī* (narrator) to be a reliable person while as a matter of fact he was not."

It is further stated in the *Tadhkirat al-Ḥuffāẓ* that Abū Bakr, addressing a meeting of the Muslims, said: "You relate from the Prophet *aḥādīth* and you differ from one another in the narration of these traditions. People after you will differ much more. Therefore do not narrate anything from the Prophet in future. If anyone asks you a question, tell him that you have the Book of God with you. What He has validated is valid and what He has invalidated is invalid."

During the time of the *Khilāfat-i Rāshidah*, *Ḥadīth* collections were destroyed for the third time. The *Ṭabaqāt* says that several such collections were prepared by people in the time of 'Umar. He ordered those people to bring the collections to him and, when they were brought to him, he ordered that they be burnt. It is said in *Jāmi' Bayān al-'Ilm* that 'Umar himself at one time intended to reduce the *aḥādīth* into writing. He consulted the Companions of the Prophet on the point and they advised him to do so. He continued to think over the matter for a month and then, one morning, he said: 'I had a mind to prepare a *Ḥadīth* collection. But then I remembered that people before us wrote books and got so much absorbed in them that they put aside the revealed Books. By God, I would not allow this to happen to the Qur'ān.' "

'Umar was so strict in this matter that whenever he appointed a governor for a place outside Arabia, he used to direct him not to narrate too many *aḥādīth*. He once gave three days' imprisonment to Ibn Mas'ūd, Abū al-Dardā' and Abū Mas'ūd Anṣārī, well-known Companions of the Prophet, on the ground that they had narrated too many *aḥādīth*. Abū Hurairah, the most exuberant narrator of *aḥādīth*, was once asked if he had been narrating many traditions in 'Umar's time. He replied that if he had done so, he would have been flogged by 'Umar.

'Umar was very cautious in accepting *aḥādīth* as well. He acted on a tradition only if the narrator was supported by two witnesses. It is said in the *Muwaṭṭā'* of Imām Mālik that when Abū Mūsā al-Ash'arī, a well-known Companion, related a *ḥadīth* in the presence of 'Umar, he asked him to produce witnesses in his support or he would punish him. 'Alī, though not as stringent as 'Umar, used to ask the narrator to narrate the *ḥadīth* on oath before it could be accepted.

During the *Khilāfat-i Rāshidah* only a very small number of *aḥādīth* were in circulation. The Caliphs themselves were very slow in narrating these traditions. Out of hundreds of thousands of *aḥādīth* which are current today, only about one hundred traditions have come down to us through Abū Bakr. The same is the case with 'Umar. From 'Alī, as well, only a very small number of *ṣaḥīḥ* traditions can be found in our *Ḥadīth* collections.

According to the *Ṣaḥīḥ Bukhārī*, Sha'bī says: "Ḥasan Baṣrī, though one of the *Tābi'īn*, narrates too many *aḥādīth*; I have been with Ibn 'Umar (a *Ṣaḥābi*), for two years and during this period he related only one *ḥadīth*." We have it on the same authority that 'Abdullah b. Zubair says : "I once asked Zubair why I had not heard him relating *aḥādīth* while so and so narrated many of them. Zubair replied that, though he had always been with the Prophet, he was reluctant to relate *aḥādīth* because he had heard the Prophet say: 'He who tells lies on me should seek his abode in Hell'." On the face of it, Zubair has suggested that these copious narrators are liars. Bukhārī mentions Anas as well as having said the same thing.

Present Ḥadīth Collections. With this background in the early years of Islam, we come now to the question of the compilation of the voluminous *Ḥadīth* collections which we have with us today. When and under what circumstances this work was taken in hand is an important and interesting study. Throughout the first century of the Hijrī era and the first quarter of the second century no attempt to collect *Ḥadith* in book form seems to have been made. The *Sunnah* remained unwritten. During the time of the Companions of the Prophet, i.e. the *Ṣaḥābah*, and the Companions of the Companions of the Prophet, i.e. the *Tābiʻīn*, it was the living and not the written *Sunnah* that ruled. The words and the acts of the Prophet and his Companions, as far as they were generally known, were, with the Qur'ān, the sole guiding principles to regulate the lives of the believers. There were no books with them for the purpose, excepting the Qur'ān. The more learned *Ṣaḥābah* and (after them) the *Tābiʻīn* acted as lawyers, jurists and judges for all law cases that arose. During the *Tābiʻī* period seven lawyers known in legal literature as the *Fuqahā'-i Sabʻah* wielded great authority in the field of law, at different places to which they belonged. They are: (1) Sa'īd b. Musayyib (d. after 90/707), (2) 'Urwah b. Zubair (d. 94/711), (3) Abū Bakr b. 'Abd al-Raḥman (d. 94/711), (4) 'Ubaidullah b. 'Abdullah b. 'Utbah (d. 94 or 98/711 or 716), (5) Khārijah b. Zaid (d. 99 or 100/717 or 718), (6) Sulaimān b. Yaṣār (d. about 100/718) and (7) Qāsim b. Muḥammad (d. 106/724).

It was by the end of the *Tābi'ī* period that people like Zuhrī, Rabī' and Sa'īd began to compile *Ḥadīth* collections. Ibn Juraij in Mecca, Auzā'ī in Syria, Sufyān Thaurī in Kūfah and Ḥammād b. Salamah in Baṣrah wrote books on the subject. They wrote what they heard and never cared to see if it was authentic.

Muwaṭṭā'. For the first time in this history Imām Mālik (93-179/710-795) made a fairly reliable collection of traditions, known as the *Muwaṭṭā'*. The book is very popular throughout the Muslim world. The Imām was one of the *Taba' Tābi'īn*. *Muwaṭṭā'* is the only *Ḥadīth* collection coming down to us from one of the four Imāms who founded the four schools of Sunnī Law. Mālik had not compiled his collection in a volume; his disciples did this after him and prepared copies from it. The original collection had ten thousand traditions, but Mālik made a selection and in its final form the *Muwaṭṭā'* contained only 1720 traditions, out of which 822 come down from the Prophet, 613 from the *Ṣaḥābah* and 285 from the *Tabi'īn*.

Musnads of the Three Imāms. The collection known as *Musnad Abū Ḥanīfah* is not the work of Abū Ḥanīfah (80-150/699-767). It was compiled by Qāḍī Abul-Muayyid Khwārazmī in the year 674/1275. The *Musnad* of Imām Aḥmad b. Ḥanbal (164-241/779-

855), which is the most voluminous of all the *Ḥadīth* collections, contains about 40,000 traditions. But it is generally believed that it is the work of the Imām's son and Abū Bakr Qaṭī'ī and others. Curious stories are in circulation about this *Musnad.* It is said that Aḥmad selected this collection from 7,50,000 traditions which all he had committed to memory. What a wonderful memory, indeed! But this is not all. According to the *Ṭabaqāt al-Kubrā* by Shaikh al-Islām Tāj al-Dīn Subkī (d. 771/1369), 'Abdullah the son of Imām Aḥmad says that his father had reduced into writing ten million traditions and he could repeat all of them from memory. How unfortunate it is that some of us believe in the truth of these and even more absurd stories. Likewise, the collection attributed to Imām Shāfi'ī (150-204/767-819) known as the *Musnad Shāfi'ī* is not his work. It was compiled by Muḥammad b. Ya'qūb al-Aṣamm on the authority of Rabī' b. Sulaimān, a pupil of Shāfi'ī.

Ṣiḥāḥ Sittah. But the most popular and reliable and very extensively used *Ḥadīth* collections are the *Ṣiḥāḥ Sittah*, i.e. the six *ṣaḥīḥ* books. They were compiled by Bukhārī (d. 256/870), Muslim (d. 261/875), Abū Dāwūd (d. 275/888), Tirmidhī (d. 279/892), Nasā'ī (d. 303/915) and Ibn Mājah (d. 273/886). The six compilers lived and worked in the third century Hijri era, mostly in the second half of it. They do not base their collections on any older work of the kind. They claim to have received the traditions from a series of transmitters, the *rāvīs*, who reproduced these traditions from memory. In other words, all the *aḥādīth* in these collections came down from man to man and so on. The number of years, about two and a half centuries, between the original source, the Prophet, and the compilers, Bukhārī and Muslim, and others definitely show that the chains of transmitters must have been considerably long. The *isnād*, i.e. the chain of *rāvis* for the very first *ḥadīth* given in *Ṣaḥīḥ Bukhārī* would be sufficient to illustrate the proposition. Bukhārī says:

حدثنا الحميدى قال حدثنا سفيان قال حدثنا يحيى بن سعيد الانصارى قال اخبرنى محمد بن ابراهيم التيمى انه سمع علقمة بن وقاص الليثى يقول سمعت عمر بن الخطاب رضى الله عنه على المنبر قال سمعت رسول الله صلى الله عليه وسلم يقول انما الاعمال بالنيات ـ

["I was told by Ḥumaidī who said that he was told by Sufyān who said that he was told by Yaḥyā b. Sa'īd al-Anṣārī who said that he was informed by Muḥammad b. Ibrāhīm al-Taimī that he heard 'Alqamah b. Waqqāṣ al-Laithī saying that he heard 'Umar b. al-Khaṭṭāb saying on a pulpit that he had heard the Prophet saying that actions are judged in accordance with the intentions with which they are done. . . ."]

Each individual in such chains generally represents a different generation as in a pedigree table like this:

The Prophet
|
'Umar b. al-Khaṭṭāb
|
'Alqamah b. Waqqāṣ al-Laithī
|
Muḥammad b. Ibrāhīm al-Taimī
|
Yaḥyā b. Sa'īd al-Anṣārī
|
Sufyān
|
Ḥumaidī
|
Bukhārī

We see that between the Prophet and Bukhārī there are six transmitters in this chain. Now the question naturally arises whether it would be perfectly safe to trust six different persons and six different memories belonging to different generations extending over about two hundred and fifty years.

There are about three thousand *aḥādīth* in Bukhārī but, including the repetitions, the number would be almost double. It is stated that Bukhārī selected these traditions from seven lakhs of such traditions which he had actually received. The same is the case with Muslim and Abū Dāwūd, and others. There are innumerable transmitters through whom these *aḥādīth* came down to the compilers of the *Ṣiḥāḥ Sittah*. It cannot be denied that the six writers, especially Bukhārī and Muslim, worked very hard, very carefully and very honestly in making their selections from millions of traditions that had come down to them. Bukhārī had made and framed certain conditions for the acceptance of a tradition to be included in his *Ṣaḥiḥ* and he followed those rules very strictly. But the task had insurmountable difficulties. Scrutiny into the life, character and reliability of each and every transmitter was made and several books on the subject were written by different scholars, from time to time. But from the nature of the work, this investigation could not be anything more than a superficial examination, because biographies of these numerous narrators have never been available at any time, and we have already referred to the evidence of Abū Bakr that some of the *Ṣaḥābah* even could not be trusted in this respect.

Other Ḥadīth Collections. Moreover, apart from

the *Ṣiḥāḥ Sittah*, we have got a large number of other *Ḥadīth* collections as well, which were not compiled with much care and caution and were made long after the *Ṣiḥāḥ*. Some of these works are fairly popular and extensively used as sources of law. The collections by Baihaqī, Ṭaḥāwī, Ṭabarānī, Dāraquṭnī and Ḥākim and others belong to this category. These compilers actually wrote down whatever they heard and never cared to see whether a tradition was good and authentic or otherwise. The collection of Ibn ʻAsākir, Jauzaqānī and Khwārazmī and others are full of the sayings of philosophers and highly exaggerated versions of simple little facts by professional preachers and sermonisers, in the garb of *aḥādīth* coming down from the Prophet himself.

It would be idle, therefore, to suggest that we should undemurringly accept all the alleged *aḥādīth* appearing in any collection. We have a right to scrutinise and examine in detail every tradition that comes before us, before accepting it as a source of law on any point. I am sure the Muslim intelligentsia of today would under no circumstances agree with those jurists who say that people of the first four centuries of the Hijri era have done all the necessary scrutiny for us and we are bound by the results of their investigations. In the words of Iqbal (*Payām-i Mashriq* [*Kulliyāt*], p. 60/230) :

میان آب و گل خلوت گزیدم   ز افلاطون و فارابی بریدم
نکردم از کسے دریوزۂ چشم   جہاں را جز بچشم خود ندیدم

we have every right to see things for ourselves and with our own eyes.

Waḍʻ Ḥadīth. The position becomes more serious

when we see that there is a fairly large number of fabricated *aḥādīth* in *Ḥādīth* collections. Ibn Jauzī (d. 597/1199) asserts that forged *aḥādīth* can be found even in the *Ṣaḥiḥ Bukhārī* and *Ṣaḥiḥ Muslim*, the two most reliable collections. The following are the main causes of *waḍ' ḥadīth*, i.e. fabrication of traditions, according to Ibn Ḥajar 'Asqalānī (d. 852/1448):

(*a*) Faithlessness in the garb of Islam, like that of the *zanādiqah*;

(*b*) Extreme ignorance like that of some over-pious people;

(*c*) Sectarian prejudices;

(*d*) Selfishness of certain rulers and magnates, and

(*e*) Love of notoriety.

The *zindīqs* were the greatest criminals in this respect. They were enemies of Islam, but in outward appearance they lived like true Muslims. They were 'Ajamīs mostly. One of these people named 'Abd al-Karīm was tried on a charge of forging traditions and sentenced to death. At the time of his execution he said that he had already accomplished his object and fabricated four thousand *aḥādīth* and disseminated them throughout the Muslim world. Equally or even more dangerous forgers were some over-pious people who invented many persuasive and deterrent and awe-inspiring *aḥādīth* with the object of making people more God-fearing. The Muslim mystics, the sufis, belong to this class. Some of these good folk have gone so far as to assert that it is lawful to forge such *aḥādīth* with such a purpose. It has been remarked by Yaḥyā ibn Sa'īd Qaṭṭān: "I have never seen a bigger forger and liar than some people who are generally known to be pious." Forgeries of this class were readily accepted with the result that our books on *taṣawwuf* are full of these spurious traditions. The works of Imām Ghazālī (d. 505/1111) as well contain a considerable number of such counterfeit *aḥādīth*. Sectarian prejudices were responsible for the largest number of false traditions. After the death of the Prophet, the Muslims were, unfortunately, divided into different political sects. During the time of 'Alī these sects further multiplied. The followers of these sects wantonly manufactured *aḥādīth* in support of their respective causes. These sects even today extensively use these alleged sayings of the Prophet in support of their views and against one another. The followers of the different schools of law forged traditions in support of their view-points. *Aḥādīth* in support of different ruling dynasties and individuals can also be found in large numbers in our *Ḥadīth* collections.

Isnād. Even in the case of those traditions which are generally considered to be true and genuine, the *isnād*, i.e. the chain of transmitters, as has already been remarked, is bound to be long, owing to the fact that the work of the compilation of traditions began very late in Muslim history. For example, the *Musnad* of Imām Aḥmad, which is one of the earlier compilations, gives the *isnād* for a tradition in the following way: Aḥmad from Shāfi'ī, Shāfi'ī from Mālik, Mālik from Zahrī, Zahrī from 'Abd al-Raḥmān, 'Abd al-Raḥmān from his father Ka'b and Ka'b from the Prophet. The longer the chain, the more difficult it is to make a satisfactory inquiry into the reliability of all the individuals concerned. Of course, much valuable work has been done in this respect in the *Ṭabaqāt* by Dhahabī, the *Kitāb al-Ḍu'afā'* by Nasā'ī, the *Iṣābah* by Ibn Ḥajar and the *Usud al-Ghābah* by Ibn Athīr, and others, but the inquiries made by these writers are necessarily inadequate.

Apart from this, the rules applicable to these inquiries were defective, e.g. the following rules:

(1) A notorious liar becomes a reliable narrator after he repents.

(2) A person telling lies occasionally is a reliable narrator.

(3) All *Ṣaḥābah* were reliable narrators.

(4) A person who takes money for narrating traditions is a reliable narrator and his *aḥādīth* may be included in the collections.

Contradictory Traditions. We have, as well, a large number of *aḥādīth* which contradict each other. Such traditions are found in the *Ṣiḥāḥ Sittah* as well. The only safe course in these cases is the well-known principle that: اذا تعارضا تساقطا ["When two traditions contradict each other, they cancel each other"], but our jurists have in most of such cases made futile and sometimes ridiculous attempts at harmonising interpretations with a view to reconciling them. These attempts have in fact adversely affected the simplicity and clearness of so many legal propositions. Contradictory versions of many historical events go a long way to prove the unreliability of many of the narrators. A few instances would suffice to illustrate the point. The number of Muslim soldiers concerned in the Tabūk expedition was, according to one *riwāyat*, 30,000, according to another 40,000, according to the third 70,000 and according to the fourth one lakh. The number of Muslims gathered at Ḥudaibīyyah was 700, 1300, 1400, 1500 1525, 1600 and 1700 according to seven different narrators. And both Tabūk and Ḥudaibīyyah are very important events in Muslim history and they are mentioned in the Qur'ān itself in detail. But the most surprising instance is that there are different *riwāyats* about the date of the death of the Prophet himself.

Binding Force of Ḥadīth. No Muslim can deny that a genuine *ḥadīth* as a source of law has, after the Qur'ān, the greatest binding force for all Muslims irrespective of their sects and schools. But, unfortunately, the followers of one sect would, in most cases, refuse to accept a tradition narrated by the followers of the other sect, without taking the trouble of finding out whether the tradition is true or false. According to the *Tadhkirat al-Ḥuffāẓ*, Bukhārī would not take a tradition coming down through Ja'far Ṣādiq although the majority of the Muslims would accept it. On the other hand, "the Shī'ahs reject not only the decisions of the oecumenical councils, but also all traditions not handed down by 'Alī or his immediate descendants." So is the case with other sects.

As a matter of fact the earlier Ḥanafīs never paid much attention to the *Ḥadīth* traditions. Almost all the *Muḥaddithīn* were non-Ḥanafīs. It is said in the well-known History written by Ibn Khaldūn that Abū Ḥanīfah, the Imām A'ẓam, himself knew only seventeen *aḥādīth*. This, at least, suggests that the number of *aḥādīth* in circulation at the time was not at all large. The later jurists of the Ḥanafī school of law, of course, developed traditionalism to a great extent.

There are many kinds of *aḥādīth*. But considering *isnād* only, *aḥādīth* are divided into three categories :

(1) *Mutawātir*, which means a *ḥadīth* which was narrated by a large number of the *Ṣaḥābah* and later by a large number of the *Tābi'īn* and then in their time by a large number of the *Taba' Tābi'īn* and so on to the time when it reached the compilers. Such a *ḥadīth* is rightly believed to be a genuine one.

(2) *Mashhūr*, which means a *ḥadīth* which was not *mutawātir* in the beginning but became so later on.

(3) *Khabar Wāḥid* (pl. *aḥād*), which means a *ḥadīth* which was narrated throughout its history and throughout its chain of transmitters by one narrator only. This is the weakest kind of *ḥadīth* as far as the strength of *isnād* goes.

It is deplorable that many of our jurists hold that a *ḥadīth* can abrogate a mandate of the Qur'ān itself. Some of them have said that a *khabar wāḥid.* cannot repeal the Qur'ān, but others hold that a *ḥadīth* of this kind may as well repeal a Qur'ānic verse. This is man-worship. 'Umar foresaw it and it was, therefore, that he burnt the *Ḥadīth* collections made during his time. According to the Shī'ah doctrine, the oral precepts are in their nature supplementary to the Quranic ordinances, and their binding effect depends on the degree of harmony existing between them and the laws of the Qur'ān. The opinion of Imām Abū Yūsuf (d. 182/798) is the last word on the subject. He says that a tradition which goes against the Qur'ān could not possibly have come down from the Prophet.

Naẓar-o 'Iyān Test. The question whether the commonsense test can be applicable to the case of an inquiry into the genuineness of a *ḥadīth* has been replied by some in the affirmative and by others in the negative. A minority of our writers who believe in the freedom of thought say that if a *ḥadīth* is against *naẓar-o 'iyān*, i.e. against reason and common-sense or an obvious and manifest reality and observation, it should be rejected forthwith, without going into the soundness of the *isnād.* But the more orthodox people who are in majority would not agree to it. They hold that our religion is based on *naql*, i.e. traditions, and *'aql* has no place in it. God forbid, if this were true we would all be dubbed fools.

All Traditions Are Not Law. Before taking a *ḥadith* as the basis of law we must always have the following facts in view:

(1) Ibn 'Abbās says that the Prophet at times acted in a particular way just by chance. This could not be law for us.

(2) He also says that some acts of the Prophet were done for reasons which existed only for the time being. They could not be the *Sunnah*.

(3) Some decisions of the Prophet were made in a particular case with its particular circumstances. The narrator mistook it as a precedent for all cases.

(4) Zaid says that some orders of the Prophet were just by way of advice. They could not be law for us.

(5) Some acts of the Prophet were done by habit. These cannot be called *Sunnah*.

(6) Some orders of the Prophet were only directory. The narrator took them as mandatory.

(7) Some prohibitory orders of the Prophet were by way of *Nahī Tanzīhī*, i.e. it is advisable not to do it, but they did not make the thing unlawful.

(3) *Ijmā'*. And now we come to *Ijmā'*, the third source of Muslim Law. It is third on the list and third in authority. In theory at least, we can have recourse to it only in case the point of law is not covered by the first two sources. *Ijmā'* has been defined differently by different jurists. *Al-Manār*

calls it the *Ijmā' al-Ummah*, i.e. the consensus of the general body of Muslims called the *Sawād-i A'ẓam*. According to the author of the *Nūr al-Anwār*, the consensus of the people of Medina, the consensus of the *Ahl-i Bait* or the consensus of the *Ṣaḥābah*, and others would come under the definition of *Ijmā'*. Sufyān Thaurī says that a *Faqih* living at the top of a mountain may constitute the *Sawād-i A'ẓam* and his opinion may have the force of *Ijmā'*. *Isḥāq* b. Rāhwaih (d. 230/844) was once asked what *Sawād-i A'ẓam* meant. He replied : "Muḥammad b. Aslam and his followers." Some people have defined the word as the consensus of scholars which is the same thing as the *Opinion prudentium* of the Roman Law. The word has also been defined as "the general usage of the community which has been established by agreement in the larger circles of believers independent of tradition or inferred law." Sir 'Abdur Raḥīm defines *Ijmā'* as the agreement of the jurists among the followers of the Prophet in a particular age on a particular question. Ameer Ali defines *Ijmā'* in the following words: "*Ijmā'-i Ummat* implies general concordance. Under this collective name are included all the apostolic laws, the explanations, glosses, and decisions of the leading disciples of the Prophet, especially of the first four caliphs (*Khulafā'-i Rāshidin*) on theological, civil and criminal matters."

Most of our jurists say that if we find a genuine *ḥadith* against the *Ijmā'*, we will follow the *Ijmā'* on the presumption that this *ḥadith* has been repealed by another *ḥadith* though we do not know it. Some of the Mu'tazilah have gone so far as to say that *Ijmā'* can repeal a Quranic ordinance as well.

On the other hand, some jurists seem to refuse to recognise the authority of *Ijmā‘* as a source of law. Shāfi‘ī is reported to have said : "*Ijmā‘* ? What is *Ijmā‘* ? The opinion of those whom we do not even know ?" And there are those as well who would deny the very existence of *Ijmā‘*. Generally speaking, the word implies the unanimous opinion of the scholars of a particular age on a point of law. Imām Aḥmad b. Ḥanbal says : "The claim of *Ijmā‘* is a lie. How can we know that the scholars were unanimous on the point ? There may have been those who differed." Most of the jurists would not accept an *Ijmā‘* which is not based on the Qur'ān or the *Ḥadith*. "The Sunnīs regard the concordant decisions of the successive Caliphs and of the general assemblies as supplementing the Quranic rules and regulations and as almost equal to them in authority."

It is noteworthy that the force of *Ijmā‘* as an authority, whether it be the opinion of all the jurists or some of them or even one of them, has always been recognised by all the known systems of jurisprudence, Muslim and non-Muslim.

(4) *Qiyās*. The fourth and the most disputed source of law is *Qiyās*. "It means the deduction of legal prescriptions from the Qur'ān and the *Sunnah* by reasoning by analogy." It involves the investigation of the '*Illat al-Shar‘*, i.e. the motive of law, the *ratio legis*, and the application of the reasoning in one case to the facts of the other case. The first three sources of law form the basis of this fourth source. Some jurists would place *Qiyās* before *Ijmā‘*

because *Ijmā'* as well uses *Qiyās*. Thus *Qiyās* comes both before and after *Ijmā'*. Therefore the division made in the list of sources is not very logical.

It may be noted here that *Qiyās* like *Ijmā'* is recognised as a source of law by all systems of jurisprudence. Salmond, the well-known British jurist, says:

> "When the decision is not on authority the judge takes recourse to . . . analogy of pre-existing law. From a comparative study of provisions of law for analogous cases, the judge may deduce a new principle and apply it if it appeals to be just or reasonable according to natural justice."

As has been said above, there has been great difference of opinion among jurists belonging to the different schools of law, on the authority attached to *Qiyās* as a source of law. Independent thinkers like Abū Ḥanīfah and his disciples use *Qiyās* very freely, some use it sparingly and others would not at all recognise it as a source of law. As a matter of fact, *Qiyās* forms the principal point of difference among the four subdivisions of the Sunnī school of jurisprudence. The jurists who are in favour of *Qiyās* have cited several instances in which the Prophet himself used *Qiyās* in deciding law cases which came before him. Instances of the use of *Qiyās* have been cited even from the Qur'ān itself.

On the other hand, as we have already seen, some jurists include *Qiyās* in the list of the sources of law very reluctantly. Shāfi'ī says that *Qiyās* can be resorted to only when it is unavoidable. Imām Aḥmad b. Ḥanbal says that even a *ḍa'īf ḥadīth* against which there are serious doubts, e.g. by reason of its contents or one of its *rāvīs* is considered unreliable or not quite orthodox, would have preference over *Qiyās*. The Ẓāhirīs or literalists (followers of Abū Dāwūd Sulaimān) have disapproved of analogical deductions and rejected that mode of proceeding. They say that there could not possibly be any case for which law has not been given in the Qur'ān or the *Sunnah*. Among the most violent opponents of *Qiyās* is Yaḥyā b. Aktham (d. 242/856), the celebrated Shāfi'ī and *qāḍī* of Baghdad under Māmūn. He wrote a book, *Kitāb al-Tanbīh*, which is wholly devoted to an attack on the Iraq school of law which uses *Qiyās* extensively.

(5) *Rā'i*. The fifth source of law, which is not on the list, is *Rā'i*, i.e. independent opinion. Once again, it is the Ḥanafī jurists who are the greatest advocates of this outlawed source of law. They rely on the *ḥadīth* which tells us how the Prophet, when he sent Mu'ādh b. Jabal to the Yemen as a *qāḍī*, asked him : "How will you decide when a question arises ?" He replied : "According to the Book of Allah." "And if you do not find the answer in the Book of Allah ?" "Then according to the *Sunnah* of the Messenger of Allah." "And if you do not find the answer either in the *Sunnah* or in the Book ?" "Then I shall come to a decision according to my own opinion without hesitation." Then the Prophet patted Mu'ādh on the chest with his hand saying : "Praise be to Allah Who has led the messenger of the Messenger of Allah to an answer that pleased him." This *ḥadīth* can be found in Abū Dāwūd, Tirmidhī, Dārimī, and others.

The fact is that to ban independent opinion is to ban all progress and development, not only in matters of law but also in all other spheres of life.

The *Ṣaḥābah* (Companions of the Prophet) used to decide cases according to their own opinion when they could not find any authority on the point in question from the Qur'ān and the *Ḥadīth*. According to a tradition found in *Sunan* of Dārimī, Abū Bakr used to decide cases on the authority of the Qur'ān, the *Sunnah*, the opinion of his friends and his own opinion. 'Umar as well followed the same course. Ibn 'Abbās used to follow the *Kitāb*, the *Sunnah*, the law given by Abū Bakr and 'Umar and his own opinion. According to *Tafsīr Ṭabarī*, Mu'āwiyah once applied to Zaid b. Thābit on a legal question on which neither he nor other Companions could quote any authority from the Qur'ān and the *Sunnah*; the latter gave a verdict based on his own independent opinion. The *Qāḍī* of Egypt asked the advice of Caliph 'Umar II (d. 101/719) on a point not provided for in Traditions. The *Qāḍī* wrote to him : "Nothing has reached me in this matter, therefore I leave it to you to give verdict according to your opinion."

Ḥammād b. Abī Sulaimān was the first to gather a circle of scholars around him whom he taught a system of *Fiqh* in which *Rā'i* had a predominant influence. To this school belonged Abū Ḥanīfah.

But there has always been a hostile minority who would not agree to be bound by the opinion of any mortal, excepting the Prophet himself. They believe that God and the Prophet had provided legislation for all contingencies that might ever arise.

Shāfi'ī (d. 204/819) was a mediator between the two extremes and he created the science of the use of *Ḥadīth* and *Rā'i*, etc. There again developed a tendency to overemphasise *Fiqh* based on *Ḥadīth* in the school of Aḥmad b. Ḥanbal (d. 241/846).

This controversy further subdivided our jurists into two sects, the *Aṣḥāb al-Rā'i* and the *Ahl-i Ḥadīth*. The subdivision persists even to this day.

(6) *Istiḥsān*. The sixth source of Muslim Law (which is not on the list but is in force in practice) is *Istiḥsān*. To quote the *Encyclopaedia of Islam*, "This is the name given to a method of argument used in the Ḥanafī school to settle *Fiqh* rules in conformity with the requirements of everyday life, equity or social conditions. The object of *Istiḥsān* is much the same as that of *Istiṣlāḥ* applied in the Mālikī school. According to both methods, the results of *Qiyās* were often simply disregarded, when it was considered necessary or simply desirable to depart from the strict demands of theory.... *Istiḥsān* and *Istiṣlāḥ* are objected to by many and have never been generally recognized as reliable fundamentals in the science of law (the *uṣūl al-fiqh*)."

The requirements of everyday life and advisability, i.e. *Maṣliḥat* are the two determining principles of *Istiḥsān* and *Istiṣlāḥ*. Several instances of the use of *Istiḥsān* are found in the *Sunnah* itself. According to a *ḥadīth* given in the *Ṣaḥīḥ Bukhārī*, the Prophet had forbidden the use of the pots in which wine had ever been stored. But when people told him that this would mean a great hardship to them, because they could not afford to purchase new pots, he withdrew the prohibition. According to the same authority, the Prophet ordered the Muslims to prepare *nabīdh* only in skins, but when he was told that many people had no skins with them, he allowed them the use of pitchers for the purpose.

The well-known and the standard text-book on Ḥanafī Law, the *Hidāyah*, very frequently mentions law points which have been determined according to *Istiḥsān* as against the conclusions arrived at by the analogical process.

But Shāfi'ī is very much against this process of argument and says: "He who uses *Istiḥsān* claims to be a law-maker."

(7) *Old Laws.* Old laws, God-given and man-made, are the seventh source of Muslim Law. Some of our jurists have mentioned these laws in this connection, but they would not like to give them prominence by entering them in the list. The *Nūr al-Anwār* says: "Old laws given by God or by the Prophets are binding on us if they are mentioned in the Qur'ān or the *Ḥadīth* and not amended or repealed by them. For example, the law of murder and hurt given in the Taurāt ('life for life and eye for eye . . .') and mentioned in the Qur'ān [ان النفس بالنفس و العين بالعين] is binding on us." The circumcision rite practised by the Muslims is as well a part of the Biblical law. The prohibited degrees of consanguinity and affinity for purposes of marriage given in the Qur'ān are exactly the same as given in the Old Testament with just one or two changes. What has been said about intoxicants in the Qur'ān is almost the same as said in the Bible. As a matter of fact, we can find hundreds of Biblical verses reproduced in the Qur'ān both on questions of faith and rites and of law. Some of the laws given by the Prophet as well can be traced back to the same source.

(8) *Custom.* We now come to the eighth source of Muslim Law, i.e. the old customs and laws of the

Jāhilī Arabia and the countries conquered by the Muslims. The great work, the *Ḥujjat Allah al-Bālighah* by the great Muslim writer and theologian, Shāh Walīullah says:

"On matters relating to marriage, divorce, commerce, social dealings, government, crimes and inheritance, etc., Islam did not give such laws to people as were absolutely unknown to them. Such laws would have made them miserable. What Islam did was to amend the old laws wherever it was necessary to remove their defects. . . . In the time of 'Abd al-Muṭṭalib, blood-money was fixed at ten camels. But when he saw that this was not sufficiently deterrent he raised it to one hundred camels. The Prophet retained it as the law for the Muslims. The rule of *Qasāmat* applicable to murder cases in Muslim Law was first made by Abū Ṭālib. According to the *Jāhilī* law, the head of the tribe used to get one-fourth of the war booty as his share. The Prophet reduced it to one-fifth. The Iranian king Kaiqubād and his son Nūshīrwān had imposed *Kharāj* and tithe as State taxes. These were retained by the Prophet with very minor changes. . . . The customs of a people are the heart of their body politic. Islam, like all other religions, directly and immediately examined them and, after necessary amendments, retained them. The *Namāz*, the *Wuḍū*, the *Sijdah* and *Zakāt* were known to and practised by the *Jāhilī* Arabs. Islam made amendments in their procedure and retained them. *Ḥajj* as well was not something new to the Arabs. They also observed the sanctity of the *Ashhar al-Ḥarām*, the sacred months, in which fighting was prohibited. . . . Apart from the local laws and customs of *Jāhilī* Arabs, some of the laws of the Persian and Roman Empires, which had been adopted by the Arabs were also retained by the Prophet after they were examined and considered by him."

In the words of Ameer Ali, "Considering the close proximity of the two nations and their frequent contact in schools and colleges, as in the field and in the Hall, it is impossible to suppose that Byzantine ideas exercised no influence on the legal conceptions of the Arabian jurists." Sir Abdur Raḥīm says: "The ground work of the Muhammadan legal system, like that of other legal systems, is to be found in the customs and usages of the people among whom it grew and developed." Tyabji holds that "the legal position of the Qur'ān must be compared to an Amending Act rather than to a complete code. The real substratum was the existing customary law of the Arabs." The *Fuṣūl-i 'Imādīyyah* cites several jurists who say: "There are many law points which were decided by our predecessors according to the habits and customs of the place where they lived. Those decisions are not necessarily good law for every judge and for every place; every case should be decided in the light of the usages of the time and place." The *Khānīyyah* holds the same view. We come across law points which have been determined according to customs almost in every chapter of the *Hidāyah*. And yet our jurists would not like to enter custom in the list of the sources of Muslim Law.

Chapter 2

THE FOUR SCHOOLS OF MUSLIM (SUNNĪ) LAW

Background. During the time of the Companions of the Prophet (the *Ṣaḥābah*). Muslim jurisprudence was not a special science or art or subject. Consequently, there was no occasion, then, for hair-splitting, niceties or complicated and far-fetched arguments on points of law. These things, along with the formation of different schools of thought and the different sects with sectarian prejudices, party spirit and bigotry, crop up only when any branch of knowledge assumes the shape of a special science or art.

During all this period, which covers more than one half of the first century of the Hijri era, the *Ṣaḥābah* acted as judges throughout the Muslim Empire. They had with them no written code of substantive or adjective law, excepting the Qur'ān itself. The other main source of guidance for them was the unwritten living *Sunnah.* Beyond the limits of Arabia, the local laws and customs of the people were also recognised, to a considerable extent, as enforceable, as long as they did not override the express dictates of the Holy Book or the *Ḥadīth.* Whenever and wherever it was found necessary, the judges freely exercised their independent opinion and discretion in all matters of detail relating to law points which arose for decision in cases pending before them.

It is interesting to note that during this period of our legal history, free thinking was not banned ; and everybody, big or small, learned or illiterate, had the right to express his own opinion on a point of law and to differ from anyone else, whosoever and whatsoever he may be. Just one out of the numerous instances recorded in our juristic annals would suffice to illustrate the point. 'Umar the Great was one day delivering his *khuṭbāh* to a congregation when he said : "If I learn that the amount of dower fixed for any woman is greater than the amount of dower fixed for the wives of the Prophet, I shall cut down the excess without hesitation." On this a woman stood up and said : "By God, 'Umar, you have no right to do so, because the Qur'ān says :

وَآتَيْتُمْ إِحْدَاهُنَّ قِنطَارًا فَلَا تَأْخُذُوا مِنْهُ شَيْئًا

['And (if) ye have given unto one of them (in dower) a sum of money however great (say a heap of gold), take back nothing from it' (iv. 20)].

On this 'Umar said to the congregation : "Is it not wonderful that your *Imām*, the Amīr al-Mū'minīn went the wrong way and a woman went the right way. She debated the question with him and won ?"

This healthy spirit of free discussion, forbearance and recognition of the right of private judgment in legal and religious matters and the liberty to uphold one's opinion went down intact to the next generation, the age of the *Tābi'īn*, the companions of the Companions of the Holy Prophet. During this period, the seven jurists, Sa'īd b. Musayyib and 'Urwah, and others known in the history of Muslim Law as the *Fuqahā'-i Sabah*, were the main exponents of both the temporal and the spiritual laws for the Muslim world of the times. Of course, they differed from one another on many questions of detail in matters of law, but it should be remembered that this difference of opinion never took the form of seven distinct and definite schools of jurisprudence. These lawyers passed away between the years 90 and 106 of the Hijri era. During the *Tābi'ī* period, as well, no attempt at the codification of Muslim Law was made. The *Ṣaḥābah* and the *Tābi'īn* seem to have been too busy otherwise to be able to find time for writing books.

It was during the *Taba' Tābi'īn* period, i.e. the period of the companions of the companions of the Companions of the Holy Prophet, that we find, for the first time in the history of our jurisprudence, attempts at a semblance of the codification of our laws. According to the *Encyclopaedia of Islam*, "E. Griffini has recently discovered among the South Arabian treasures of the Ambrosian library in Milan a compendium of *Fiqh* attributed to the founder of the Shī'ah sect of the Zaidiyah, entitled as the *Majmū'ah* of Zaid bin 'Alī (d. 122 H.). This would be the oldest attempt at a codification of Muslim Law in existence; in any case it is to be reckoned with the literature of the older *Fiqh*. If it should be a direct product of the circle of Zaid bin 'Alī himself, we should have to recognize the priority of the Shī'ah (Zaidī) branch of Islam in *Fiqh* literature among the works that have survived. It has not yet, however, been fully investigated what position this collection holds in the history of *Fiqh* literature."

Before the *Madhāhib-i Arba'ah* came into existence, we do hear of the Hejaz school and the Iraq school of Muslim Law, in our legal literature. We find mention of other schools of law as well, e.g. the school of Auzā'ī, of Sufyān Thaurī, of Ṭabarī and the Ẓāhirī school, but all these disappeared from the field after a short existence. These so-called schools never assumed any exactly defined shape, although it cannot be denied that they exercised a very great influence in the matter of the shaping of the present four schools of Sunnī Law.

Madhāhib-i Arba'ah. These schools are popularly known as the *Madhāhib-i Arba'ah*, i.e. the four *madhhabs*. It must be borne in mind that the word *madhhab*, as it is used here, does not mean "religion". Here it has its simple etymological meaning, i.e. a "way," a "path". Therefore, the *Madhāhib-i Arba'ah* are in no sense four religions, only utter ignorance could call them four sects even. The difference between these four schools of Muslim Law is only the difference of opinion on certain questions of detail in legal propositions. It should always be remembered that all through the first three centuries of the Hijri era, difference of opinion was considered to be a sign of life and a source of blessing. It has been said that اختلاف ائمة الهدى توسعة للناس, i.e. the difference of opinion among the leaders provides amplitude for the followers. Thus we see that if a Ḥanafī judge finds that in the circumstances of a particular case a decision according to Ḥanafī law would create great hardship to a party, he may decide the case according to the Mālikī, the Ḥanbalī or the Shāfi'ī law, and this latitude is available for the judges of all these schools. As a matter of fact, the *Madhāhib-i Arba'ah* have, throughout the Muslim history, been represented in all the great centres of Islam by judicial functionaries who used to decide important law cases at a joint conference. At the Jāmi'at al-Azhar, the most important University of the Muslim world of today, all the four systems of Muslim jurisprudence are represented by both the teachers and the students. The Mecca Mosque has four *muṣallās* for the four schools. Therefore it would be preposterous to allege that the *Ahl-i Sunnat wa Jamā'at* who form an overwhelming majority of the Muslims of the world are divided into four sects. And as far as law is concerned, excepting, of course, the constitutional law and some aspects of the law of marriage, the differences in law between the Shī'ahs and the Sunnīs are also scarcely more considerable than the differences between the Sunnī schools of law.

(1) *Ḥanafī School.* I propose to deal with the *Madhāhib-i Arba'ah* in their chronological order. The first in this order is the Ḥanafī school. It was founded by Imām Abū Ḥanīfah, al-Nu'mān Thābit b. Zūṭa b. Māh, popularly known as *Imām-i A'ẓam.* His grandfather Ibn Zūṭa was brought to Kufah from Persia as a slave by the Muslim conquerors, where he was purchased and later liberated by a woman of Banī Taimullah tribe and was thus the *maulā* (i.e. a client) of that tribe. Zūṭa embraced Islam and his son Thābit, the father of Abū Ḥanīfah, was born in Islam, as a member of the Banī Taimullah. But Ismā'īl b. Ḥammād, the grandson of Abū Ḥanīfah, says that the grandfather of the Imām was never a slave. He also gives his name as Marzbān and not Zūṭa. However, the statement of Ismā'īl has never been generally accepted.

The Imām-i A'ẓam was born in the year 80/699. His

father Thābit was forty years old at that time. It has been stated on the authority of Ismā'īl b. Ḥammād, that Thābit, when a baby, was taken to Amīr al-Mū'minīn 'Alī who blessed him and his descendants. The *Encyclopaedia of Islam* on the authority of Imām Nawawī and the *Sīrat al-Nu'mān* by Shiblī, have credited this story which has been narrated by several historians, but some of the *Mutakallimīn* say that the story is highly improbable.

It has been said that Abū Ḥanīfah spent some years of his early life under the care of Imām Ja'far Ṣādiq and was educated by him. But he got his *Fiqh* from Ḥammād b. Abī Sulaimān, one of the most eminent teachers of Muslim Law at the time. The Hejaz school of thought during that period did recognise the validity of *Rā'i* (personal opinion) as a source of law, to a considerable extent, but the Iraq school excelled them in many ways, in this respect. Ḥammād b. Abī Sulaiman (d. 120/738) is said to be the first teacher who gathered around him a circle of scholars to whom he taught the system of law in which *Rā'i* had a predominant influence. Abū Ḥanīfah belonged to this school and he and his disciples worked so forcefully on these lines that the Muslim jurists got divided into two distinct groups known as the *Ahl-i Ḥadīth* and the *Aṣḥāb-i Rā'i*. These groups exist even today.

Abū Ḥanīfah was a well-off man. He was a cloth merchant and did good business in that line. He devoted all his life to the study of law. It is generally believed that he never wrote anything himself. Some small books like *Fiqh-i Akbar* which carry his name as their author are said to have been compiled by his disciples and his grandson Ḥammād. He as a teacher imparted knowledge to his pupils by way of discussions. Whenever a question of law arose, Imām-i A'ẓam held discussions and debates with his students on the point. He and the students used to cite whatever authority on the point they had in the form of *ḥadīth* or the opinions of the *Ṣaḥābah*, etc. These discussions were so exhaustive and in detail that in some cases just one proposition remained under discussion for several days and even for a month. At the end of the discussion the question and the decision thereon were reduced to writing by one of the disciples of the Imām. During these debates the Imām-i A'ẓam never insisted on the correctness of his opinion in the case. On several occasions he withdrew his opinion frankly admitting it to be wrong and accepted the opinion of one of his pupils. Out of a very big circle of his students, the most learned are Imām Abū Yūsuf, Imām Muḥammad, Imām Zufar and Imām Ḥasan, who are as much responsible for the present shape of Ḥanafī jurisprudence as the Imām-i A'ẓam himself. The four disciples differ from their master on many legal propositions. The validity of free and independent thinking and liberality, inspired by the Imām-i A'ẓam, is so patent in the Ḥanafi school that the later jurists of the school have, in many cases, accepted and acted upon the opinion of one of the four disciples as against the opinion of the Imām-i A'ẓam. The names of the four disciples as given above are in the order of their importance, their learning and the force which their opinions carry. A perusal of the *Hidāyah*, the most popular text-book of Ḥanafī law, would show that on a large number of law points the unanimity of Abū Yūsuf and Muḥammad, known in Ḥanafī legal literature as the *Ṣaḥīḥain* carries greater weight than the opinion of Abū Ḥanīfah himself. In some cases the opinion of Muḥammad is accepted as against the opinion of Abū Yūsuf. We find in the same book instances of Zufar being followed as against the majority of Ḥanafī jurists. Therefore it is abundantly clear that the Ḥanafī jurists of old cared more for convincing arguments than for personalities. Imām-i A'ẓam himself has said: "If you find stronger arguments against my opinion, follow those arguments and not my opinion."

It is a moot question whether Abu Ḥanīfah was a *Tabi'ī* or not, i.e. whether he had met and heard from a *Ṣaḥābi* or not. It is believed that a few *Ṣaḥābis* were alive when he was a small boy. But the generally accepted opinion is that Abū Ḥanifah was not a *Tābi'ī*; he was one of the *Taba' Tābi'īn*.

Some people who are not very great admirers of Imām-i A'ẓam say about him: ان بضاعته فى العربيه كانت مزجلة, i.e. his knowledge of the Arabic language and literature was meagre and wanting in fullness. But this is something which these people feel pleased to say about many eminent scholars, writers and poets. The *Ahl-i Ḥadīth* say the same thing about his knowledge of the *Ḥadīth*. Anyhow, it has never been denied that he is the greatest jurist throughout the history of Muslim Law. His power of legal reasoning was so great that Imām Mālik once said: "If you talk to him about this wooden pillar and ask him to prove that it is made of pure gold, he would be able to do so by the force of his arguments." What Mālik actually meant by saying so matters little, the fact remains that Abū Ḥanīfah's reasons for his legal dictums are generally very convincing.

The following is a brief statement of the special features of the legal system founded by Abū Ḥanīfah:

(1) He used the *Ḥadīth* as the basis for legal propositions very sparingly. He was not the type of a man who would be prepared to accept all *aḥādīth* that reached him without thorough scrutiny. Moreover, there were no written collections of these traditions at that time. Long after him, when such collections were compiled in large numbers, the later Ḥanafī jurists began to use them in law books written by them. But even they do not follow these traditions as unhesitatingly as some other schools of law and the *Ahl-i Ḥadīth* do.

(2) Abū Ḥanīfah and his followers base most of their legal propositions on *Qiyās* which means the deduction of legal prescriptions from the Qur'ān, the *Ḥadīth* and the *Ijmā'* by reasoning or analogy. The other three schools of law do recognise *Qiyās* as a source of Muslim Law, but they do not use it so frequently. According to Ibn Khallīkān, Shafi'ī (who was one of Mālik's disciples) relates an interesting story of a dialogue between himself and Muḥammad (the disciple of Abū Ḥanīfah) relating to Abū Ḥanīfah's *Qiyās*:

Muḥammad to Shāfi'ī: "Who is more learned, my master, Abū Ḥanīfah or your master, Mālik?"

Shāfi'ī: "Justly and truthfully ?"

Muḥammad: "Yes."

Shāfi'ī: "God is witness! Who is more learned in the *Kitāb*, my master or your master ?"

Muḥammad : "By God, your master."

Shāfi'ī : God is witness. Who is more learned in *Sunnah*, my master or your master ?"

Muḥammad : "By God, your master."

Shāfi'ī : "God is witness. Who is more learned in the *Ijmā'* of *Ṣaḥābah*, my master or your master ?"

Muḥammad : "By God, your master."

Shāfi'ī : "Then there remains nothing but *Qiyās*, and *Qiyās* must be based on the *Kitāb*, the *Sunnah* and the *Ijmā'*. Now tell me, what does your master base his *Qiyās* on ?"

(3) Abū Ḥanīfah was the greatest advocate of the validity of free and independent personal opinion as one of the sources of Muslim Law and it is, therefore, that Ḥanafī jurists are called the Aṣḥāb-i Rā'i. The other three schools did not entirely disclaim the use of *Rā'i* but made a moderate use of it in comparison with the Ḥanafī school. There has always existed a minority which refuses to recognise *Rā'i* as a proper basis for the deduction of laws They regard this legal skill as an idle abuse of law. There were also people who believed that the Qur'ān and the *Ḥadīth* have provided legislation for all the law points that may ever arise and that, therefore, the question of the validity of personal opinion as a source of law did not arise at all.

(4) Apart from the four generally recognised sources of Muslim Law, Abū Ḥanīfah has another method of argument, known as *Istiḥsān* used to settle legal rules in conformity with the requirements of everyday life, equity or social conditions. According to his method, the results of *Qiyās* are often disregarded when considered necessary or desirable. Numerous

instances of legal propositions based on *Istiḥsān*, where the conclusions arrived at by *Qiyās* were disregarded can be found in the *Hidāyah*. Moreover, the Ḥanafī school recognises the validity of basing legal propositions on local customs and the general practice of the people of a place, unless they go against the letter or the spirit of the *Kitāb* or the *Sunnah*. Shāh Walīullah Dihlawī, in one of his small but useful books entitled the *'Iqd al-Jīd*, quotes several eminent jurists saying that a *Muftī* should be well acquainted with the habits and customs of the people of his town because our jurists of the past answered many question of law in the light of the general practices of their people.

A careful and critical study of Muslim Law would show beyond the shadow of a doubt that a large number of details in our laws are based on the habits, customs and old pre-Islamic laws of the countries conquered by the Muslims.

(5) But the most distinctive feature of the Ḥanafī jurisprudence is its liberality and munificence. Some ungenerous people belonging to other schools of law have been actually ridiculing Abū Ḥanīfah for this characteristic of his *Fiqh*. It is one of the principles of interpretation according to the British jurisprudence that fiscal law should be interpreted, as far as possible, in favour of the subjects. Abū Ḥanīfah interprets all laws in favour of man. He would never agree to any proposition of law based on an interpretation which causes undue hardship to anyone. He is known for his permissions and facilities, usually called *Rukhṣathā'-i Abū Ḥanīfah*. The writers of the East and West all agree that he erected a very tolerant

system of law in which he made the greatest concession to the methods of *Qiyās*, *Rā'i* and *Ta'āmul* (i.e. habitual practices). Abū Ḥanīfah was a free thinker and he never failed to apply the commonsense test to all the legal deductions he made. He never lost sight of reason in any matter. His *Fiqh* is more sensible, judicious and moderate and much easier to follow than the *Fiqh* of any other school. This seems to be one of the main reasons why an overwhelming majority of the Sunnī Muslims of the world follow the Ḥanafī school. 'Allāmah Ibn 'Abd al-Barr, in his well-known took the *Jām' Bayān al-'Ilm*, cites a *ḥadīth* according to which the Prophet said : "The best religion is the easiest religion."

It would not be out of place, I suppose, to give here some instances to illustrate this aspect of the Ḥanafī school in comparison with other schools.

(*a*) In the opinion of the Imām-i A'ẓam, a Muslim may say his prescribed prayers in his own language, using as well the translation of the Quranic verses, the recitation of which is compulsory therein, even if he is able to say prayers in Arabic. The *Ṣāḥibain*, i.e. Abū Yūsuf and Muḥammad, who could not go so far as their master has gone, say that a person who is unable to say his *namāz* in Arabic may say it in his own language, but not otherwise. According to the *Talwīḥ*, a standard work on Muslim jurisprudence, and the *Durr-i Mukhtār*, a popular text-book of Ḥanafī Law, Nūḥ b. Maryam says that the Imām-i A'ẓam later changed his opinion and accepted the opinion of the *Ṣāḥibain* as correct. But this seems to be an attempt to save Abū Ḥanīfah from the scathing criticism levelled against him by some people, on this score. No other school of law would accept a prayer said in a language other than Arabic as valid under any circamstances. We see that the later Ḥanafī jurists fell in line with other schools of law in this respect by and by, because we have never heard of any Muslim saying his *namāz* in his mother tongue.

(*b*) Another very interesting case is that of *khamr*, (i.e. *sharāb*). The use of *khamr*, as you know, is prohibited by the Qur'ān:

انما الخمر و الميسر و الانصاب و الإزلام رجس من عمل الشيطان فاجتنبو ـ

["Strong drink and games of chance and idols and divining arrows are only an infamy of Satan's handiwork. So shun it" (v. 90-91).]

The *Nūr al-Anwār*, a commentary on Nasafī's *Al-Manār*, a standard work on Ḥanafī jurisprudence, gives the views of the Imām-i A'ẓam on this point in the following words: "*Khamr* is the name of an intoxicant made from grapes by a particular process. Therefore, all other intoxicants made from figs, dates, wheat or honey, etc., or made from grapes by some other process are not *khamr* and the Quranic ordinance relating to *khamr* cannot apply to them. Taking into consideration the '*illat al-shara*', that is the motive of law or the *ratio legis*, we find that the use of *khamr* is prohibited because it intoxicates a man. It follows that the use of any other intoxicant would be a sin and a punishable offence only in case it is taken in a quantity which causes intoxication, while the use of *khamr* even to the extent of a single minim is sinful and punishable." On the other hand, Shāfi'ī, Mālik, Aḥmad and Muḥammad say that all intoxicants are *khamr* and are governed by the rules applicable to it. Most of the later Ḥanafī jurists have shown a definite leaning towards the view of the other three schools on this point.

(*c*) According to the Qur'ān, the punishment prescribed for theft is the amputation of the hand of the thief. Abū Ḥanīfah considers this punishment as the maximum punishment for the offence. Therefore, he would not cut off the hand of the thief in many petty and less serious cases of theft. On the other hand, other schools of law consider amputation as the only punishment for theft and would order that a hand of the thief be cut off in almost all cases of theft.

(*d*) In the opinion of Abū Ḥanīfah, if a person in a dark night makes a wrong guess as to the *Qiblah* direction and says his prayer facing the wrong direction, his *namāz* would be good and he need not say it over again on learning of his mistake. Shāfi'ī would have the prayer said over again.

(*e*) According to Shāfi'ī, ablution, i.e. *wuḍū*, cannot be performed with the water which has been heated on dung-cake fire. He also prohibits the use of the food cooked in an earthen pot on that fire. He declares the use of *pashmīnah* cloth, *samūr* and *postīn* as unlawful and says that the *namāz* said in these garments is no *namāz*. He would not allow the use of utensils and furniture, etc., with silver work on them. According to him, a *dhimmī* is not a competent witness in any case, not even in cases relating to transactions between the *dhimmīs* themselves. Imām-i A'ẓam differs from Imām Shāfi'ī in all these matters.

Innumerable instances of the kind can be found in books of Muslim Law. No one can deny that Abū Ḥanīfah is very liberal in his views and is never unduly strict in any matter. His laws are not the laws for over-pious people only. He built up a system of jurisprudence for the average man in a society which was definitely growing and developing in all aspects of a social and civilised life.

A big majority of the Sunnī Muslims of the world follow the Ḥanafī school. The other three schools divide the minority between themselves. An impartial student of Muslim Law would, with no difficulty, be able to find out the reasons for the popularity of the Ḥanafī jurisprudence, by a comparative study of the laws of the four schools. Sufyān b. 'Uyainah says that at first it was thought that the opinion of Abū Ḥanīfah on points of law would not cross the Basrah bridge but in no time it spread to the boundaries of the Muslim world. The uncharitable remarks of Ibn Ḥazm that the schools of Abū Ḥanīfah and Mālik owe their popularity to State patronage has no foundation. It is true that Abū Yūsuf was appointed the Chief Qāḍī of Baghdad and held this office till his death in 182/798, under the three 'Abbāsī Caliphs, Mahdī, Hādī and Hārūn Rashīd. But we know that no Muslim ruler has ever had any prejudice against any school of law. All the four schools have been equally respected in every place and in every age and have had equal facilities and opportunities for the propagation of their systems.

Abū Yūsuf wrote several books on Ḥanafī Law. His well-known book *Kharāj* on land-tax was dedicated to Hārūn Rashīd. He used to dictate legal propositions to his students who belonged to different parts of the Muslim Empire and thereby gave wide publication to the views of Abū Ḥanīfah on law points.

Muḥammad, as well, worked on the same lines as Abū Yūsuf. It can, therefore, be safely asserted that the *Ṣāḥibain* with the Imām-i A'ẓam were jointly responsible for the construction and the publication of the Ḥanafī system of Muslim jurisprudence. But all the same it is impossible to agree with the cruel remarks of 'Ammār b. Abī Mālik that if Abū Yūsuf was not there no one would have heard of Abū Ḥanīfah. Of the later Ḥanafī jurists Ṭaḥāwī, Karkhī, Qudūrī, Burhān-ud-Dīn Marghinānī and Abū al-Barakāt Nasafī are the most important. It is worth noticing that none of the great traditionists, i.e. the *Muḥaddithīn*, was a Ḥanafī.

We have already seen that Abū Ḥanīfah was a colth merchant and a well-to-do man. Unlike his two disciples, the *Ṣāḥibain*, he was never in government service. During the time of Marwān b. Muḥammad, the last ruler of the Banī Umayyah dynasty, Yazīd b. 'Umar b. Ḥubairah, the governor of 'Irāqain, offered him the post of *Qāḍī* at Kufah and had given him whipping for his refusal to accept it. Later when Manṣūr became the Khalīfah and made Baghdad his capital, he sent for Abū Ḥanīfah and offered him the post of *Qāḍī* of Baghdad. Abū Ḥanīfah refused to accept the offer. Manṣūr was annoyed and said: "I swear in the name of God that I will make you the *Qāḍī*." Abū Ḥanīfah replied: "I swear in the name of God that I will *never* accept the post." On this Manṣūr sent him to prison. This was in 146/763. In the prison, the Imām was a detenu more than a prisoner. All due respect was shown to him there. His students were allowed to go to him daily for their lessons. His second best disciple, Imām Muḥammad, got most of his education in this prison college. It is generally believed that the Imām-i A'ẓam was really detained for reasons of State. He had been a supporter of Ibrāhīm, the well-known political adversary of Manṣūr. Moreover, the pupils of the Imām held different posts and positions throughout the Empire, in large numbers. He was loved and respected everywhere and had great influence over the learned classes of Baghdad itself. Such widespread popularity of an individual has always made the Eastern monarchs uneasy. Abū Ḥanīfah died within the four walls of the prison in 150/763.

The Ḥanafī school is followed in Pakistan, India, Afghanistan, Turkistan and the rest of Muslim Central Asia, Turkey, Arabia, the greater part of Egypt and parts of other Arabia countries.

(2) *Mālikī School.* Now we come to the Mālikī school founded by Imām Abū 'Abd Allah Mālik b. Anas b. Mālik b. Abī 'Āmir b. 'Amr b. al-Ḥārith b. Ghaimān b. Khuthail b. 'Amr b. al-Ḥārith al-Aṣbaḥī. He came from the Ḥimyar tribe who are included in the Banū Taim b. Murrah Quraish and belonged to Medina. The exact date of his birth is not known. He was born between 90/708 and 97/716. Dhahabī says: "Abū 'Āmir, the great-grandfather of Mālik, was a contemporary of the Holy Prophet, but has nowhere been mentioned as a *Ṣaḥābī*." Mālik himself was definitely one of the *Taba'-i Tābi'īn*. It has been said that he learnt *Fiqh* from Rābī'ah b. Farrukh who cultivated *Rā'i* in Medina and is, therefore, usually known as *Rabī'at al-Rā'i*. According to Ibn Khallikān, Mālik had learned *Qirat* from Nāfi' b. Abī Nu'aim. He got his *ḥadīth* traditions from a large number of

Tābi'īn and the *Taba'-i Tābi'īn* including Zuhrī, Nāfi' Maulā Ibn 'Umar, 'Abd Allah b. Dīnār, Abū Zinād, Hāshim b. 'Urwah and Muḥammad b. Munkadir and others. Mālik himself says that he got most of his learning from people who came to ask *fatwās* from him and not from his teachers.

The greatest work of his life is the *Muwaṭṭā* which is a collection of traditions coming down from the Prophet, the Companions of the Prophet and the Companions of the Companions of the Prophet. Thus the book is a compendium of the *Ḥadīth*, the living *Sunnah* and the *Ijmā'* and the general practice of the Muslims of Medina. The traditions given in the *Muwaṭṭā* are arranged subject-wise, like text-books of codified laws. It is said to be the earliest surviving Muslim law book. As a matter of fact, in transmitting the *Muwaṭṭā*, Mālik did not make a definitive text in a volume. His pupils prepared different editions of it, as they heard it from him. These *Riwāyāt* (recensions) of the *Muwaṭṭā*, in places, differ very much from each other. The *Bustān al-Muḥaddithīn* enumerates and describes sixteen such recensions of the *Muwaṭṭā*. The *Encyclopaedia of Islam* mentions fifteen recensions and says that only two of these still survive in their entirety. One of them is the *Muwaṭṭā* as edited by Muḥammad b. al-Ḥasan al-Shaibānī. It may be noted that this Muḥammad is the same Muḥammad as already mentioned as a disciple of Abū Ḥanīfah. Muḥammad had been a student of both these *Imāms*. Al-Shaibānī, at the end of most chapters of his edition, gives his own views and that of Abū Ḥanīfah on questions discussed, sometimes with very full reasoning. It is this edition which is mostly in use in Pakistan and India. The other edition is the *Muwaṭṭā* as transmitted by Yaḥyā b. Yaḥyā al-Maṣmūdī, a disciple of Mālik. This edition is also in use in this subcontinent.

The following are the special features of the Mālikī School of Law :

(*a*) As pointed out by Shāh 'Abd al-'Azīz Muḥaddith Dihlwī, out of the four founders of the *Madhāhib-i Arba'ah* Imām Mālik alone has to his credit a collection of *Ḥadīth* traditions. Such collections attributed to the other three *Imāms* were actually made by their pupils after and, in some cases, very long after them. But it cannot be said that *Ḥadīth* was the only court of appeal for Mālik. He used to give preference to the *'amal* or *ta'āmul*, i.e. the actual practice in Medina over the traditions when they differed from each other. In his opinion, general practice of the Muslims of the city represented the living *Sunnah* and was, therefore, more reliable than verbal traditions.

(*b*) Not much different from Abū Ḥanīfah's *Istiḥsān*, Mālik had his method of *Istiṣlāḥ* to settle legal rules in conformity with the requirements of everyday life and equity. According to both these methods, the results of *Qiyas* were in some cases ignored when it was found necessary or desirable to do so. These methods have not been recognised as valid sources of law by several jurists.

(*c*) Mālik is not against *Rā'i*. He did exercise *Rā'i* in cases in which Medina tradition or Medina *Ijmā'* did not exist. As a matter of fact, he has been reproached, by some people with agreement with the 'Irāqīs on this point. Ibn Khallikān relates a legend according to which Mālik repented of his exercise of *Rā'i* on his death-bed. But this seems to be a story made by the anti-*Rā'i* biographers of Mālik, with the purpose of showing that they are justified in their views against the use of *Rā'i* in legal matters.

But it should be remembered that Mālik exercised *Rā'i* very sparingly. He had never diverged to any considerable extent from his Medina contemporaries in his views about *Rā'i*. He used to criticise Abū Ḥanīfah very severely for his free exercise of *Rā'i*. For example, 'Abd Allah b. Muslimah Qarshī tells us that Imām Mālik used to say that things went on very well till Abū Ḥanīfah came and put *Rā'i* in vogue amongst the Muslims. Khālid b. Nazār attributes much stronger words to Mālik in this connection· According to him, Mālik once said: "If Abū Ḥanīfah had attacked the Muslims with a sword in his hand he would not have injured them as much as he did armed with his *Rā'i* and *Qiyās*." The Medina jurists, including Mālik, though they never rejected *Qiyās* absolutely, did not give it the importance which Abū Ḥanīfah gave it.

Mālik was very much against forcing his own code of law on people. Once Khalīfah Abū Ja'far Manṣūr told him that he intended to send copies of the *Muwaṭṭā* to all important cities in the Muslim Empire and order that judges should follow that book exclusively and ignore other sources. Mālik prevented the Khalīfah from doing so and told him that people in different parts of the Empire were following traditions which had reached them and they should not, therefore, be disturbed at all.

Once 'Abd al-Raḥmān b. Qāsim told Mālik that the people of Egypt were experts in the law relating to sales. Mālik wanted to know the reasons for it. 'Abd al-Raḥmān said : "They are experts because they follow you." Mālik replied : "I do not know much of the law of sale myself ; how could they become experts in that law by following me ?"

As in the case of Abū Ḥanīfah, so in the case of Mālik, Ibn Ḥazm, the versatile Spanish Arab scholar, says that the Mālikī school owed its popularity in Spain to State patronage, because, Yaḥyā b. Yaḥyā, the disciple of Mālik, was a great favourite of the King of Spain and all the appointments of judges were made through him. But all the other historians of Islam say that the Mālikī school got a hold on Spain through the numerous pilgrims of that country who visited Medina and went back full of praises for Mālik for his piety and eminence in learning.

Mālik, when a student, was a very poor man. Later he became extremely rich through the patronage of his admirers both in the royalty and the nobility and gentry.

Hārūn Rashīd once requested Imām Mālik to come to the palace and narrate the traditions of the *Muwaṭṭā* to his children. Mālik replied : "People come after knowledge, not knowledge after people." The princes used to go to the school of Mālik, in the mosque, after that.

Ibn Jauzī says that in the year 147/764 Mālik got a whipping for having given a *fatwā* against the wishes of the Sulṭān.

At present the Mālikī school is followed in parts of Upper Egypt and West Africa.

Among Mālik's pupils may be mentioned Laith b. Sa'd, 'Abdullah b. Wahb and Ma'ān b. 'Īsā and others.

Of the later Mālikī jurists, 'Abd Allah b. Abī Zaid Qairawānī, author of the *Risālah*, and Khālid b. Isḥāq of the *Mukhtaṣar* are well known.

Mālik died in the year 179/795.

(3) *Shāfi'ī School.* The third in the chronological order is the Shāfi'ī school founded by Imām Abū 'Abd Allah Muḥammad b. Idrīs b. 'Abbās b. 'Uthmān b. Shāfi'ī b. Sā'ib. The Imām belonged to the tribe of Quraish and was a Hāshimī and thus remotely connected with the Prophet. Sā'ib, the grandfather of his great-grandfather, was a *Ṣaḥābī*. Both the Imām and his followers are popularly known as Shāfi'ī.

Shāfi'ī was born in the year 150/767, the year of Abū Ḥanīfah's death. The historians have recorded an interesting anecdote in this connection. A Ḥanafī said to a Shāfi'ī : "Your master did not dare to come to the world as long as my master was there." Shāfi'ī replied : "No, that is not the case. The truth is that when my master came to the field, your master ran away."

The place of Shāfi'ī's birth is not exactly known. Some historians say he was born at Ghazzah, others say at 'Asqalān. Yemen and Minā as well are mentioned as his places of birth. But it is certain that he was brought up in Mecca, by his mother, in very humble circumstances.

Shāfi'ī spent a considerable time with the Beduins and acquired a thorough knowledge of the *Jāhilī* Arab poets. He studied *Fiqh* with Muslim b. Khālid Zinjī (d. 180/796) and Sufyān b. 'Uyainah (d. 198/814). He knew *Muwaṭṭā* by heart at the age of fifteen. He was about twenty when he went to Medina to Imām

Mālik and remained there as long as Mālik was alive. After the death of Mālik, he went to Yemen where he took an appointment. Here he was involved in a political intrigue and was brought a prisoner to Hārūn Rashīd. He was pardoned and then became intimate with Muḥammad b. Ḥasan Shaibānī (the well-known disciple of Abū Ḥanīfah) whose books he had copied for himself.

In 188/804, Shāfi'ī went via Ḥarrān and Syria to Egypt where he was well received as a pupil of Mālik. He went to Baghdad in 195/810 where a large number of scholars gathered round him and he set up successfully as a teacher there. His earlier books were written here. He returned to Mecca and after some time again went to Baghdad. This time he spent only a month there and left for Egypt. Most of his books, the *Kitāb al-Umm*, the *Imlā'-i Ṣaghir*, the *Mukhtaṣar* and the *Risālah*, etc., were written in Egypt.

It has been generally recognised that Shāfi'ī was the first jurist of Islam who wrote books on *Uṣūl-i Fiqh*, i.e. jurisprudence, on scientific lines. His works were actually compiled, arranged and published by his pupils. It is, therefore, that the different editions of his books differ from one another on many points, for example, the *Mukhtaṣar* has three editions, known as the *Mukhtaṣar Buwaiṭī*. the *Mukhtaṣar Muzanī*, and the *Mukhtaṣar Rabī'*, named after his pupils. The *Umm* (printed at Cairo in seven volumes) is actually a collection of Shāfi'ī's smaller works which Baihaqī mentions as separate books.

Shāfi'ī's life was devoted to reading and teaching. He had a wonderful memory. He never forgot anything. Muḥammad, the well-known disciple of Abū

Ḥanīfah, tells us that once Shāfi'ī borrowed Abū Ḥanīfah's book the *Ausāṭ* from him and committed it to memory in one night and one day. Muslim historians have recorded some other memory feats of Shāfi'ī as well.

One of the more prominent features of Shāfi'ī's jurisprudence is the fact that he selected such doctrines as pleased him in every school and borrowed freely from various sources. He was not exclusive in opinion. We have already seen that Abū Ḥanīfah, his disciples and other 'Irāqī jurists made a very extensive use of *Qiyās*, *Istiḥsān* and *Rā'i*, as sources of Muslim Law. On the other hand, Mālik and most of the other Ḥijāzī lawyers would resort to these methods of deduction of legal prescriptions very reluctantly.

Shāfi'ī would not go to either of these extremes. His jurisprudence was actually a compromise between these two schools. The *Encyclopaedia of Islam* says:

"Shāfi'ī may be described as an eclectic who acted as an intermediary between the independent legal investigation and the traditionalism of his time (i.e. between *Aṣḥāb-i Rā'i* and *Ahl-i Ḥadīth*). Not only did he work through the legal material available but in his *Risālah* he also investigated the principles and methods of jurisprudence. He is regarded as the founder of the *uṣūl-i fiqh*. Unlike the Ḥanafīs he sought to lay down regular rules for *Qiyās*, while he would have nothing to do with *Istiḥsān*. The principle of *Istiḥsān* seems to have been first introduced by the later Shāfi'īs."

Shāfi'ī was a critic. A fairly large number of our jurists believe that a *ḥadīth* coming down to us through many narrators can abrogate a Quranic ordinance. Some of them have gone so far as to say that a *ḥadīth* coming down to us through only one narrator can also repeal a Quranic verse. Shāfi'ī would not agree to such a strange proposition. The *Ifādat al-Shuyūkh* mentions Kya Harasi and 'Abd al-Jabbār saying that, though Shāfi'ī is a great man, the truth is greater than him and the truth is that a *ḥadīth* may repeal a verse of the Qur'ān.

Shāfi'ī would not blindly follow *Ijmā'* even. According to him, the so-called consensus of the jurists must be thoroughly scrutinised before it is accepted. He says : "*Ijmā'*, whose *ijmā'* ? The *ijmā'* of people whom we do not know ?" He believed that the word of no man excepting the Prophet could be the last word on any point of law, not even the word of a large number of people. He used to say : هم رجال و نحن رجال ["They were men and we are men. If they could say things, we can also do so"].

The more prominent among Shāfi'ī's pupils were Muzanī, Buwaiṭī, Rabī' b. Sulaimān, Murādī, Zā'farānī, Abū Thaur, Ḥumaidī and Aḥmad b. Ḥanbal, the founder of the Ḥanbalī school.

It would be interesting to note that most of our great *Mufassirīn* and *Muḥaddithīn* were Shāfi'īs, and so were most of our eminent scholars and writers, like Abū Isḥāq Shīrāzī, Imām Ghazālī, Imām Rāfi'ī, Imām Nawawī and others. Muḥyuddīn Jīlānī, 'Mu'īnuddīn Chishtī and Shihābuddīn Suhrawardī were also Shāfi'īs.

At present, the Shāfi'ī school is followed in South Arabia, Bahrain, the Malay Archipelago, the former German East Africa and some parts of Central Asia.

Shāfi'ī died in the year 204/819.

(4) *Ḥanbalī School*. The fourth and the last on the list is the Ḥanbalī school, founded by Imām Abū

'Abd Allah Aḥmad b. Muḥammad b. Ḥanbal b. Hilāl b. Asad b. Idrīs. The Imām is popularly known as Aḥmad b. Ḥanbāl. He was born at Baghdad in 164/780. Some historians say he was born at Merv and brought to Baghdad during his infancy. He belonged to the Arab tribe of Banī Shaibān. He got his early education at Baghdad. Later, his search for knowledge took him to Kufah, Basrah, Mecca, Medina, Yemen, Syria and Jazirah, etc. He studied *Ḥadīth* and *Fiqh* with Shāfi'ī and was always with him till Shāfi'ī left for Egypt.

Aḥmad collected thousands of *aḥādīth* during his travels which he undertook mainly for this purpose. The *Musnad* of Imām Aḥmad b. Ḥanbal is virtually an encyclopaedia of *Ḥadīth*. It contains about 40,000 *aḥādīth*, but it is generally believed that the *Musnad* was compiled, after the lifetime of the Imām, by his son and Abū Bakr Qaṭī'ī and others, with the addition of several thousand traditions.

In 218/833, Qāḍī Aḥmad b. Dāwūd, one of the Mu'tazilah leaders, succeeded in convincing Māmūn al-Rashīd that the Qur'ān was *makhlūq* and not *qadīm* and Māmūn started forcing the scholars to believe in the truth of the theory of *Khalq-i Qur'ān*. Some of them went in hiding, some, to save their skin, agreed to the theory outwardly, some did believe in the correctness of the theory and others proved strong enough to refuse to agree to it. A large number of the learned people of the last category were put to death. Some of them including Imām Aḥmad were arrested and were being taken to Māmūn when, on their way, the news of Māmūn's death at Ṭarsūs reached them. Later when Mu'taṣim became the

Khalīfah, Aḥmad was sent to prison with several other acknowledged theologians because they would not profess the doctrine of the creation of the Qur'ān. Painful proceedings were instituted against them, and it was only when, under Mutawakhil, the State returned to orthodoxy that the trials of Ibn Ḥanbal ceased.

In Mutawakkil's time Aḥmad was invited to the Court on several occasions and shown all due respect. Even a pension was allowed to his family, without his knowledge. The renown of his piety, unswerving faithfulness to *Ḥadīth* and his learning had gathered round him a large number of pupils and admirers.

Aḥmad spent much more time in collecting *aḥādīth* than in the derivation of the rules of law. It is, therefore, that some of the Muslim jurists including Ṭabarī do not recognise him as a decisive authority on law. Abū 'Umar says that after the *Ṣaḥābah* and the *Ṭābi'īn*, Abū Ḥanīfah, Mālik and Shāfi'ī were the *Imāms* of Islam, and he who follows them is fortunate. He has omitted the name of Aḥmad from the list. Likewise Abū Dawūd b. Ash'ath Sijistānī says: "God's mercy on Abū Ḥanīfah : he was an Imām ; God's mercy on Mālik : he was an Imām ; God's mercy on Shāfi'ī ; he was an Imam." He, too, omits the name of Aḥmad from the list of *Imāms*. As an adherent of the Ahl-i Ḥadīth he was very indulgent to traditions and sometimes he did admit very weak traditions as the basis of his legal decisions. It would not be out of place, here, I suppose, to quote the following verses of Imām Aḥmad which relate to the comparative value of the *Ḥadīth* and the *Rā'i*.

دين النبي محمد اخبار   نعم المطية للفتى آثار
لا ترغبن عن المحبث و اهله   فالرای لیل و الحدیث نهار
و لربما جهل الفتى اثر الهدى   والشمس بازغة لها انوار

["The path of Muḥammad the Prophet is *Ḥadīth* and what a wonderful conveyance for a man are the traditions! Do not turn away from *Ḥadīth* and the Ahl-i Ḥadīth because *Rā'i* is night and the *ḥadīth* is day. And it happens in so many cases that a man goes astray from the right path, though the sun is shining and spreading light."]

The most prominent characteristic of the Ḥanbalī school is that its followers would unhesitatingly accept any *ḥadīth*, however weak it may be, as a basis for a rule of law. Imām Aḥmad himself would not pay heed to the word of 'Umar, 'Ā'ishah, 'Alī, 'Uthmān, Ṭalḥah, Abū Ayyūb, Ubayy b. Ka'b, or Ibn 'Abbās, if he could find a tradition which was against the decisions of these eminent *Ṣaḥābah*. He never conducted any inquiry worth the name about the genuineness of a tradition.

The following are the more important Ḥanbalī jurists in successive epochs : Abū al-Qāsim 'Umar al-Kharaqī, 'Abd al-'Azīz b. Ja'far, Abū al-Wafā', 'Alī b. 'Aqīl, Ibn Jauzī, Ibn Taimīyyah and Ibn Qayyim, and others. Shaikh 'Abd al-Qādir Jīlānī mentioned above as a Shāfi'ī is also said to be a Ḥanbalī.

There was a fairly good number of the followers of this school in Iraq, Egypt, Syria and Palestine, up to the eighth century of the Hijri era, but at the present time they are limited to Najd only.

The Imām died in 241/855 at Baghdad.

Chapter 3

AHLĪYYAT

Ahlīyyat in Muslim jurisprudence means: "Ability and liability" in matters of religion and of civil and criminal law. A person possessed of *ahlīyyat* is known as *Mūkallaf*. Most of the principles of law relating to the question of *ahlīyyat*, under British jurisprudence, are given effect to, on the civil side, in Chapter 2 of the Contract Act and, on the criminal side, in the chapter entitled "General Exceptions" in the Pakistan Penal Code.

The word "ability" as used above in the definition of the word "*Ahlīyyat*" stands for the words "capacity," "competency" and "power" used by British jurists in this connection on the civil side. It may be noted here that, unlike other systems of jurisprudence, Muslim jurists have discussed this subject in all its details, separately and in one place, as an independent topic.

The basic authority for all the propositions of law relating to *ahlīyyat* is the Quranic verse:

لَا يُكَلِّفُ اللّٰهُ نَفْسًا إِلَّا وُسْعَهَا

["Allah imposes not on any soul a duty beyond its scope" (ii. 286).]

'Aql, i.e. the faculty of reasoning, is the main determining factor for the proof of *ahlīyyat*, because a person cannot understand what is said to him

unless he is sufficiently rational. Reason has been created in human beings in different quantities. Individuals differ from one another in the degree of intellect they possess. Thus a small boy may reason out a proposition which a grown-up person cannot. But law presumes that maturity of understanding is attained on the attainment of majority.

Ash'arīyyah. There is difference of opinion on the point of *'aql* being the determining factor for the proof of *ahlīyyat.* The Ash'arīyyah say: "No reliance can be placed on *'aql* in the absence of knowledge of law as given by the Lawgiver and, on the other hand, knowledge of law is to be relied upon even if it is not accompanied by *'aql.* We cannot find out whether something is good or bad (virtuous or vicious) or it is obligatory or prohibited, with the help of *'aql.*"

Therefore, according to the Ash'arīyyah, *īmān* (i.e. the profession of faith) of a minor who is *'āqil* (i.e. who has attained maturity of understanding) is not effective, because the law is not binding on him. The same is the opinion of Shāfi'ī on this point. They base this proposition on the following Quranic verse :

وَمَا كُنَّا مُعَذِّبِينَ حَتَّىٰ نَبْعَثَ رَسُولًا

["Nor do We chastise until We raise (send) a messenger" (xvii. 15).]

They argue that, according to this verse, *kufr*, i.e. unbelief, is not punishable until a prophet is sent to give law to the people. It follows that knowledge of law and not *'aql* is the determining factor for the proof of *ahlīyyat.* Therefore, *īmān* of a minor is of no consequence because the law is not binding on him even though he be an *'āqil*.

Mu'tazilah. The Mu'tazilah say : " *'Aql* is the reasoning which makes 'incumbent' what it finds good and declares 'prohibited' what it finds bad, more definitely and decisively than the reasonings of law, because the reasonings of law are (only) signs and do not by themselves make things 'incumbent,' while the reasonings of *'aql* do so by themselves." They say that nothing can be accepted as proved which, though proved by the reasoning of law, is incomprehensible by *'aql*. Consequently they do not believe that man can see God with bodily eyes, nor do they believe in *'adhāb-i qabr* (chastisement in the grave) nor in *Mīzān* (the balance to weigh the deeds of men), nor in the general conditions prevailing in the life hereafter (in the sense in which they have been described in words). They rely on the following Quranic verse in this connection :

وَإِذْ قَالَ إِبْرَٰهِيمُ لِأَبِيهِ ... إِنِّىٓ أَرَىٰكَ وَقَوْمَكَ
فِى ضَلَٰلٍ مُّبِينٍ

["And when Abraham said to his father. . . : I see thee and thy people in manifest eror" (vi. 75).]

Their argument (though not a strong one) is that Abraham formed his opinion about his father and his people, by the reasoning of *'aql* and not by the reasoning of law because he was not a prophet then and had no God-given law with him, and it is therefore that he said "I see" and did not say "It has been revealed to me."

They say that "a person, who has got *'aql* but

does not use it in search for truth and, therefore, remains an unbeliever, cannot be excused. A minor who is *'āqil* is *mukallaf* and is, therefore, bound to have *īmān*, though he has no knowledge of law. A person who has not received *da'wat*, i.e. a person to whom the Divine message has not been conveyed, or, in other words, a person who does not know law, e.g. a person living in a lonely place far off from hibitation, is not excusable and is punishable if he does not have *īmān*, because the mere fact of his being *'āqil* makes him *mukallaf*. But in this case he is not bound by the rules of law in their details."

Ḥanafīyyah. According to the Ḥanafī jurists, "A person who has not received *da'wat* is not *mukallaf* although he has got *'aql*. He is excusable if he recognises neither *īmān* nor *kufr*. But if he has had sufficient time to think over matters and to study the universe which leads to a belief in its Creator and has had sufficient experience of things, he becomes a *mukallaf*. The time required for this thinking, study and experience differs in the case of each individual."

According to the Ash'arīyyah, a person, who neglects to use his *'aql* in search for truth and consequently has no faith in one God and believes in polytheism, is excusable if he has not received *da'wat*, which is the determining factor with them. As already stated, in the opinion of these jurists, the *īmān* of a minor who is *'āqil* is not effective. But the Ḥanafī view is that it is effective, because the Prophet accepted the *īmān* of several minors who embraced Islam in his lifetime, although minors are not *mukallaf* to believe. It has been said that the Ḥanafī jurists are unanimous on the point that the *īmān* of an *'āqil* minor is effective, but they are not unanimons on the point that he is not *mukallaf* to be a believer. Fakhr al-Islām and his followers say that he is not, while Abū Manṣūr al-Māturīdī and Abū Ḥanīfah say that he is. As a matter of fact, the majority of these jurists are of opinion that a minor, though an *'āqil*, is not *mukallaf*. They rely on the following *ḥadīth* :

رفع القلم عن ثلاث ـ عن الصبى حتى يحتلم ـ و عن المجنون حتى يفيق
و عن النائم حتى يستيقظ ـ

["The pen (of law) has been lifted away from three persons, from a minor till he becomes major, from an insane person till he regains sanity and from one asleep till he awakes."]

Two Kinds of Ahlīyyat. Ahlīyyat is of two kinds :

(1) The first is the *ahlīyyat-i wujūb*, i.e. the *ahlīyyat* which creates obligation. It is based on the existence of a responsibility. This kind of *ahlīyyat* cannot come into existence unless there is a valid responsibility which results in obligations for and against the person. This responsibility means the agreement which human beings made with their Creator according to the following Quranic verse :

وَإِذْ أَخَذَ رَبُّكَ مِنْ بَنِيٓ ءَادَمَ مِن ظُهُورِهِمْ ذُرِّيَّتَهُمْ
وَأَشْهَدَهُمْ عَلَىٰٓ أَنفُسِهِمْ أَلَسْتُ بِرَبِّكُمْ قَالُوا۟ بَلَىٰ شَهِدْنَآ
أَن تَقُولُوا۟ يَوْمَ ٱلْقِيَٰمَةِ إِنَّا كُنَّا عَنْ هَٰذَا غَٰفِلِينَ

["And when the Lord brought forth from the children of Adam, from their loins, their descendants, and made them bear witness about themselves: Am I not your Lord? They said: Yes; we bear witness. (That was) lest you should say on the Day of Resurrection: Lo! of this we were unaware" (vii. 172).]

When we agreed that God was our Lord we impliedly agreed that we shall be bound by all the laws given by Him, whether they created rights or duties. In this connection, reference may, as well, be made to the following Quranic verses :

وَنَفْسٍ وَمَا سَوّٰهَا ۝ فَأَلْهَمَهَا فُجُورَهَا وَتَقْوٰهَا ۝ قَدْ
أَفْلَحَ مَنْ زَكّٰهَا ۝ وَقَدْ خَابَ مَنْ دَسّٰهَا

["And by the soul and Him Who perfected, and inspired it (with conscience of) what is wrong for it and (what is) right for it, He is indeed successful who causeth it to grow, and he is indeed a failure who stunteth it" (xci. 7-10).]

In other words, the basis for this kind of *ahlīyyat* is the inner voice of a person, his conscience.

Therefore, a man is born with this basic responsibility which results in obligations for and against him.

A *janīn*, i.e. an embryo, has no responsibility which could be the basis of obligations which go against it, e.g. the liability to maintain relations or to pay the price of something purchased for it. On the other hand, it can benefit by the obligations which are for it and to its interest. For example, an embryo can have the advantage of inheritance, a will in its favour or the admission or proof of its legitimacy. Birth brings with it all the obligations whether for or against a person, i.e. whether for his benefit or against his interest. But in the case of a minor, the obligations are in some cases enforceable and in other cases not enforceable. Thus in the case of *ḥuqūq al-'ibād*, i.e. the rights of men, e.g. the payment of compensation for property damaged or destroyed by him, the payment of the sale price for the property purchased for him and the payment of maintenance allowance to his wife and relatives are obligations which are enforceable against the minor, and the payment made by his guardian shall be deemed to be payment made by him. On the other hand, a minor is not liable to *qiṣāṣ* or chastisement for an act done by him. It may be noted here that the punishment which a minor gets in school or at home is only reformatory and not in enforcement of a legal obligation.

In the case of *ḥuqūq Allah*, i.e. rights of God, the obligation of a minor exists in cases in which the discharge of the obligation can be validly demanded, e.g. the payment of *'ushr* or *kharāj*. Being taxes on the produce of land, their payment is their real purpose and the payment made by the guardian is considered as payment made by the minor. There is an element of *'ibādat*, i.e. worship, in their payment and of *'uqūbat*, i.e. chastisement on non-payment, but this element is only of a secondary nature.

The obligation, in case of a minor does not exist when the discharge of it cannot be validly demanded, e.g. pure worship and chastisements. The purpose of worship is to perform the acts of worship, and this cannot be validly demanded of a minor. And the purpose of chastisement is to punish for things said or done, and this also is not proper in the case of a child.

(2) The second kind of *ahlīyyat* is the *ahlīyyat-i adā'*, i.e. the *ahlīyyat* of performance and discharge of legal duties. It is of two kinds :

(*a*) *Ahlīyyat-i Qāṣirah*, i.e. incomplete *ahlīyyat*,

This incompleteness results from some mental or physical defect. The *ahlīyyat-i aḍā'* depends upon two powers, the power of understanding the law, i.e. the power of intellect, and the power of performing the legal duties, i.e. the power of body. A man has neither of these powers in the beginning, but he has the capacity of acquiring both of them, gradually. A minor who is *'āqil* and a major who has defective intellect possess an incomplete *ahlīyyat* of performance. The discharge of legal duties made by them would be taken as valid and effective, although they had no obligation to do so.

(*b*) *Ahlīyyat-i Kāmilah*, i.e. complete *ahlīyyat*. It is based on complete power of intellect and complete power of body. This *ahlīyyat* makes the performance of legal duties obligatory. Law presumes that maturity of understanding is attained at the age of majority.

Effectiveness of Performance Based on Ahlīyyat-i Qāṣirah. The question of the validity and effectiveness of the performance of legal duties by a person possessing *ahlīyyat-i qāṣirah* may be considered under different heads :

(*i*) In the case of *ḥuqūq Allah*, when something is patently good and can under no circumstances be considered bad, e.g. *īmān*, the profession of it by a minor who is *'āqil* would be acceptable and effective, though he is not bound to do so. As an authority for this proposition the following couplet of 'Alī has been cited :

سبقتكم الى الاسلام طرا   غلاما ما بلغت اوان حلم

["I preceded you all in embraching Islam while I was a small boy and had not attained the age of puberty."]

It has been argued that if Islam during minority were not effective, 'Alī would not have felt proud of it.

According to Shāfi'ī, Islam before the age of puberty is not effective, as far as the matters of this world are concerned. Thus a minor embracing Islam will inherit the property left by his non-Muslim parents and his non-believing wife shall not be separated from him, because deprivation from inheritance and the separation of his wife are harmful for him, although his Islam would be effective as far as matters of the next world are concerned, because that would be beneficial to him.

(*ii*) Again, in the case of *ḥuqūq Allah*, when something is patently bad and can under no circumstances be considered good, for example, *kufr* which means apostasy in this case, the renunciation of Islam by a minor of mature understanding would, according to Abū Ḥanīfah and Muḥammad, be effective, both for matters of this world and of the next. Thus his Muslim wife shall be separated from him and he shall not inherit the property left by his Muslim relatives. But, according to Abū Yūsuf and Shāfi'ī. his apostasy shall not be effective in matters of this world, because this would be harmful for him.

(*iii*) In cases other than the case of *ḥuqūq Allah*, if something is absolutely beneficial for the minor, e.g. acceptance of gift or charity, he can accept it without the consent of his guardian.

(*iv*) But if something is absolutely harmful for the minor, e.g. divorce, will, making a gift or advancing loan, etc., it would be void because it means loss of conjugal or proprietary rights to the minor. Shams al-A'immah Sarakhsī differs. In his *Uṣūl al-Fiqh* he says:

"In case of necessity, a minor's divorce would be effective. We see that when the wife of a non-Muslim minor embraces Islam, Islam is offered to the minor, and if he refuses to accept it, his wife is separated from him. Now separation is a divorce according to Abū Ḥanīfāh and Muḥammad. And if a minor renounces Islam, his Muslim wife stands separated from him and this separation is divorce according to Muḥammad. Therefose a minor's divorce when effective in one case must be effective in the other."

It is submitted that the argument of Sarakhsī is not sound. Judicial separation is the act of the judge and divorce is the act of the husband and both cannot be treated as one and the same thing for all purposes.

(*v*) There are things which are partly harmful and partly beneficial or are harmful in one case and beneficial in another, e.g. a sale. A sale transaction is said to be both *sālib*, i.e. causing loss, and *jālib*, i.e. causing gain, because in a sale there is the loss of proprietary rights and the gain of the sale price. Again, a sale transaction is a losing bargain in some cases and a profitable one in others. Now a minor can sell his property with the consent of his guardian. According to Abū Ḥanīfah, such a sale would be valid even if it is patently a losing bargain, but Abū Yūsuf and Muḥammad say that it would not be valid. According to Shāfi'ī, only the guardian can transact a sale bargain on behalf of the minor. The minor himself cannot do so.

Causes Adversely Effecting Ahlīyyat. The following are the causes which adversely effect *ahlīyyat* and either destroy it or diminish its effectiveness : (1) Minority, (2) Insanity, (3) Partial Insanity, (4) Forgetfulness, (5) Sleep, (6) Fainting Fit, (7) Illness, (8) Ignorance, (9) Intoxication, (10) Jocular Mood, (11) Foolishness, Stupidity, (12) Mistake, (13) Coercion.

(*i*) *Minority*. Some aspects of the effect of minority on *ahlīyyat* have already been discussed. It may be added here that a minor follows his parents or one of them in the matter of Islam. So, if one of his parents is a Muslim, the minor shall be considered a Muslim for the purpose of law. Thus he will inherit the property left by his Muslim relations and they will inherit the property left by him. It may be noted that inheritance between a Muslim and a non-Muslim is not possible.

A minor is not liable to punishment in *Ḥudūd*, i.e. criminal cases, in which punishment is prescribed in the *Kitāb* or the *Sunnah*, nor is he liable to *kaffārah*, i.e. penitence or atonement.

The position in this respect, according to British jurisprudence is as follows :

"Nothing is an offence which is done by a child under seven years of age [Pakistan Penal Code, Sec. 82] and nothing is an offence which is done by a child above seven years of age and under twelve, who has not attained sufficient maturity of understanding to judge of the nature and consequences of his conduct on that occasion [Pakistan Penal Code, Sec. 83]."

It may be noted here that, according to British law, a person attains majority at the age of eighteen and in some cases twenty-one years. But under Muslim Law a person becomes major at the age of puberty which "is determined by the physical signs which denote that state. Failing such signs minors of either sex are held to have reached the age of puberty on completing their fifteenth year" (Abdur Rahman, *Institutes of Mussalman Law*, Art. 566).

If the wife of a non-Muslim minor embraces Islam, separation is not ordered. At his attaining majority, Islam is offered to him and, if he refuses to accept it, separation is effected.

As a general rule of law, one cannot inherit the property left by a person whom he has killed. But if a minor kills a person, whether it is murder or culpable homicide not amounting to murder, he would inherit the property left by the deceased.

(*ii*) *Insanity*. Speaking generally, insanity and minority run parallel in their effect on *ahlīyyat*. Thus the law regarding divorce and gift, etc., by an insane person is the same as governs a minor. An insane person, as well as a minor, is not exempt from the payment of compensation for the property destroyed or damaged by him or from the responsibility of maintaining his relations or from the payment of *diyat*, i.e. blood-money.

But if the wife of an insane non-Muslim embraces Islam, Islam shall be offered to one of his parents, and in the case of non-acceptance, his wife shall be separated from him.

If a person has remained insane for a full year, he shall not be liable to pay *Zakāt* for that year. This is according to Muḥammad, but Abū Yūsuf says that even if he has remained insane for the greater part of the year, he shall be exempt from such payment. It may be noted here that *Zakāt* is a State tax according to Muslim Law and is not an individual and private act of charity. In most cases complete insanity results in complete negation of *ahlīyyat* and, therefore, the special features of law relating to *ahlīyyat-i qāṣirah* are not applicable to the case of an insane person. Section 84 of the Pakistan Penal Code says :

"Nothing is an offence which is done by a person who, at the time of doing it by reason of unsoundness of mind, is incapable of knowing the nature of the act, or that he is doing what is either wrong or contrary to law."

(*iii*) *Partial Insanity*. A person is said to be partially insane if some of his talk is the talk of a sane person and some of it is like the talk of an insane person. For all purposes, the law governing him is the law governing an *'āqil* minor. Thus his acts of worship, e.g. *namāz*, etc., and his profession of Islam shall both be effective. He can be appointed a *wakīl*, i.e. an agent for the purpose of selling another person's property and his acceptance of *hibah*, i.e. a gift, would be valid and effective. But a divorce by him shall not be valid. He cannot make a sale or a purchase without the permission of his guardian. But he would be responsible for the payment of compensation for the loss of property of another person, damaged or destroyed by him.

Such a person is not bound to perform acts of worship, nor is he liable to any punishment. Like a minor a guardian shall be appointed for him. He cannot be appointed a guardian for another person.

How minority and insanity affect the *ahlīyyat* of a person, on the civil side, can be seen in Section 11 of the Contract Act, which says :

"Every person is competent to contract who is of the age of majority according to the law to which he is subject, and who is of sound mind, and is not disqualified from contracting by any law to which he is subject."

(*iv*) *Forgetfulness.* Forgetfulness affects *ahlīyyat* but slightly. If a person forgets to perform an act of worship which is incumbent on him, he commits no sin but is liable to perform the act when he remembers it. If, due to forgetfulness, he eats or drinks something while fasting, the fast is not broken. If he forgets to recite the formula *Bismillāhi Allāhu Akbar* [In the name of God, God is great] at the time of slaughtering an animal, the slaughter would be in order.

But in the case of *ḥuqūq al-ʻibād*, forgetfulness is no excuse. Thus if a person destroys or damages the property of another person on account of forgetfulness, he shall be liable to pay compensation to the owner of the property.

(*v*) *Sleep.* Sleep is a complete negation of volition, choice or option. Therefore anything said or done by a person while asleep is of no consequence.

(*vi*) *Fainting Fit.* A person falling into a swoon loses consciousness and volition. His mental faculties arc not awake. Like sleep, this state of unconsciousness is a total negation of *ahlīyyat.*

(*vii*) *Illness.* Ordinarily, illness does not affect *ahlīyyat* in any way. But in the case of illness followed by death, i.e. *marḍ al-maut*, *ahlīyyat* is partially affected. As in the case of death, the heirs and the creditors of the deceased step in, so in the case of *marḍ al-maut*, their rights create a partial disability in the sick person and his power of alienation of his property becomes subject to those rights. Thus he cannot deal with his assets in a way as to deprive the heirs and the creditors of their legal rights. A Muslim cannot give away more than one-third of his property by will; two-thirds must be left intact for the heirs. So a person in *marḍ al-maut* cannot dispose of more than one-third of his property, nor can he alienate his property in a way as to deprive his creditors of their dues.

This disability of the sick person is not absolute during his illness. It becomes so when death occurs, but then it shall be considered to have existed since the beginning of the illness.

It may be noted here that the expenditure on the necessities of life is an exception to this rule, because it takes precedence of the rights of the heirs and the creditors. Thus if a man in *marḍ al-maut* marries and pays the usual amount of dower to his wife, the payment would be valid and good even though it deprives his heirs and creditors of their rights and dues, partially or totally.

A tradition given in the *Muwaṭṭā* of Imām Mālik and narrated by 'Amr b Sulaim Zuraqī and Abū Bakr b. Ḥazm has an important bearing on the question of both *marḍ al-maut* and minority and also on certain aspects of the law of wills. The tradition says :

> " 'Umar was informed that a boy aged ten to twelve years and belonging to the Ghassān tribe was living in Medina and was on his death-bed. His heirs were in Syria and his only relation in Medina was his paternal uncle's daughter. 'Umar said that he may make a will of his property in her favour and he did it."

(*viii*) *Ignorance*. Ignorance of fact is good excuse. For example, when a sale takes place a person who has the right of pre-emption must at once declare that he will pre-empt the sale and must, as well, bring a suit for pre-emption without delay. His failure to make the declaration or to bring the suit in good time results in the loss of his right of pre-emption. But as long as he remains ignorant of the fact of sale, the delay in making the declaration or bringing the suit does not affect his right to pre-empt the sale.

Likewise, if the contract of marriage of a minor is made by a guardian of the minor, other than the father or grandfather, the minor has the option of repudiating the marriage on attaining puberty. But the option must be exercised immediately at the appearance of the signs of puberty, otherwise the option shall be lost. But if the minor is ignorant of the fact of marriage at the time, the option may be exercised whenever the marriage becomes known to him.

But ignorance of law is no excuse. For example, in the above case if the minor fails to repudiate the marriage at the proper time on account of his ignorance of the law giving the option of puberty, the marriage shall become irrevocable.

(*ix*) *Intoxication.* Before considering the question of the effect of intoxication on *ahlīyyat*, it may be noted that, according to Abū Ḥanifah and the earlier Ḥanafī jurists, no intoxicant except *khamr* (a strong drink prepared from grapes by a particular process) is prohibited unless taken in a quantity which results in actual intoxication. According to them, an intoxicant, e.g. *bhang* and opium, etc., taken as a medicine, even though it actually intoxicates, is not prohibited. Later Ḥanafī jurists agreeing with other schools of Muslim Law, say that all intoxicants are prohibited, even a drop of them.

According to the Qur'ān, a person may eat or drink anything though prohibited, in case of extreme hunger or thirst, to avoid dire consequences.

Now, if a person takes an intoxicant which is not prohibited, e.g. if he takes an intoxicant by way of medicine, or takes an intoxicant which is prohibited, e.g. *khamr*, under coercion, or in case of extreme necessity and gets intoxicated, he loses *ahlīyyat* like a person under a fainting fit. Thus his acts and words are of no consequence.

In cases of intoxication other than the above, *ahlīyyat* is not affected. Thus if he divorces his wife, the divorce would be effective. He shall be bound by the sale or purchase made by him.

But in all cases of intoxication, the renunciation of Islam by an intoxicated person shall not take effect, because, it is said that this is a matter of faith and any *pronouncement* regarding a question of that nature, made by a person who is not in full possession of his senses, could not be effective. Likewise, a person cannot be convicted on the sole basis of his confession made during intoxication, in case of offences relating purely to *ḥuqūq Allah*, e.g. adultery, but he can be so convicted in case of offences against *ḥuqūq al-ʻibād*, e.g. a false charge of adultery against somebody or *Qiṣaṣ* cases.

The position of British jurisprudence in this respect is given in section 85 of the Pakistan Penal Code, which runs thus :

> "Nothing is an offence which is done by a person who, at the time of doing it, is, by reason of intoxication, incapable of knowing the nature of the act, or that he is doing what is either wrong or contrary to law: provided that the thing which intoxicated him was administered to him without his knowledge or against his will."

On the civil side, illustration (*b*) under section 12 of the Contract Act says :

> "A sane man, who is delirious from fever or who is so drunk that he cannot understand the terms of a contract or form a rational judgment as to its effect on his interests, cannot contract whilst such delirium or drunkenness lasts."

(*x*) *Jocular Mood*. The word used is *hazl* which means: " joking, jesting or sportive language". It is the opposite of *jidd* which means "earnestness, or seriousness". A contract made by way of *hazl* is void. But *hazl* in this case must be express; it cannot be implied.

It has been said that words amounting to divorce, manumission, or relinquishment of claim for *qiṣāṣ*, etc., are effective even if uttered by way of *hazl*. As an authority for this proposition of law. the following *ḥadīth* has been referred to :

قال رسول الله صلى الله عليه وسلم ثلث جد هز جد و هز لهن جد ۔ النکاح و الطلاق والیمین ۔

> ["The Prophet said : 'There are three things in which earnestness is earncstnes sand jesting is earnestness : marriage, divorce and oath."]

But this tradition loses much force when we see that different narrators have mentioned different things in it. One version is given above. Another version mentions : النکاح و العتاق و الیمین and yet another says : النکاح و الطلاق والرجعة.

If one talks apostasy by way of *hazl* one becomes apostate not because of one's words but because of the fact of jesting with matters of faith. The following Quranic verse is an authority for this view :

قُلْ أَبِاللَّهِ وَآيَاتِهِ وَرَسُولِهِ كُنتُمْ تَسْتَهْزِئُونَ ۝ لَا تَعْتَذِرُوا قَدْ
كَفَرْتُم بَعْدَ إِيمَانِكُمْ ۚ إِن نَّعْفُ عَن طَائِفَةٍ مِّنكُمْ

["Say : Do ye scoff at God and His signs and at His apostle? Offer not an excuse: now are ye become infidels, after your faith" (ix. 65-66).]

(*xi*) *Foolishness.* The word used here is *safah* which means foolishness, stupidity, levity, want of judgment, imprudence and lack of worldly wisdom.

For purposes of jurisprudence *safah* is defined as lavishment, squandering, extravagance and prodigality. According to the *Durr al-Mukhtār*, spending too much in charity is also *safah*.

From the above definitions of the word, it is abundantly clear that *safah*, i.e. foolishness and stupidity, does not adversely affect *ahlīyyat* in any way excepting in the matter of extravagance. A foolish person is bound by all the rules of law, and is answerable for all that he says or does. His ability and liability in all matters of civil and criminal law remain unaffected. But if he is extravagant, all his property shall be taken away from him and the State shall thenceforth manage it through its agents. This proposition of law is based on the following Quranic verse :

وَلَا تُؤْتُوا السُّفَهَاءَ أَمْوَالَكُمُ الَّتِي جَعَلَ اللَّهُ لَكُمْ قِيَامًا وَ
ارْزُقُوهُمْ فِيهَا وَاكْسُوهُمْ ۔۔۔ فَإِنْ آنَسْتُم مِّنْهُمْ رُشْدًا
فَادْفَعُوا إِلَيْهِمْ أَمْوَالَهُمْ

["And make not over 'your' (i.e. 'their') property which God has made a means of subsistence for you, to the weak of understanding and maintain them out of it and clothe them . . . then if you find in them maturity of intellect, make over to them their property" (iv. 5-6).]

These verses of the Qur'ān apply to majors as well as minors and insane persons. According to Abū Ḥanīfah, the property must be restored to the owner of it when he attains the age of twenty-five years whether he is or is not able to manage it properly. But the *Ṣāḥibain* (viz. Abū Yūsuf and Muḥammad) say that, whatever his age, the property cannot be given back to him unless he is fit to manage it well. It may be noted here that the provisions of the Court of Wards Act, in this respect, are in accordance with the opinion of the *Ṣāḥibain*. Section 5 of the Act runs :

"(2) When it appears to the Provincial Government that any landholder is...(*b*) owing to any... mental defect... or (*c*) owing to his having entered upon a course of wasteful extravagance likely to dissipate his property ; incapable of managing or unfitted to manage his affairs, the Provincial Government may make an order directing that the property of such landholder be placed under the superintendence of the Court of Wards."

Section 6 of the same Act says :

"When any landholder is a minor or a person adjudged by a competent court to be of unsound mind and incapable of managing his affairs, the Court of Wards may make an order assuming the superintendence of the property . . . of such landholder."

As long as the property remains under the management of the guardian or the Court of Wards, which acts as an agent of the State, the ward has no power of alienation over it. The *Ṣāḥibain* agree with this view. Abū Ḥanīfah differs. The Ḥanafī judges have always followed the opinion of the *Ṣāḥibain* in this matter, as against the opinion of their master.

(*xii*) *Mistake. Khaṭā'* (خطأ) or bonafide mistake made in good faith after the exercise of due care and caution exonerates a person from all liability in cases of *ḥuqūq Allah*. A *Muftī* who gives a wrong *fatwā* or a *Qāḍī* who gives a wrong judgment due to such a mistake, though he had done all that he could do to find out the truth, commits no sin. The words used here are *ba'da istifrāgh al-wusi'*. On the other hand, the *Muftī* or the *Qāḍī* gets one virtue recorded to his credit, for the efforts he has made. This proposition is based on the following *ḥadīth* :

عن عبد الله ابن عمرو و ابی هربره قال قال رسول الله صلی الله علیه وسلم
ان حکم الحاکم فاجتهدو اصاب فله اجران و اذا حکم فاجتهدو اخطاء
فله اجر واحد ـ متفق علیه (مشکوة باب العمل فی القضاء) ـ

[" Abd Allah b. 'Amr and Abū Hurairah say that the Prophet said : When the *Ḥakim* makes an order after having made efforts to come to a correct conclusion and does come to a correct conclusion, he gets two rewards and when he makes an order after having made efforts to come to a correct conclusion but comes to a mistaken conclusion, he gets one reward" (narrated by Muslim and Bukhārī).]

It may be noted here that the condition of *ba'da istifrāgh al-wusi'* in Muslim jurisprudence is exactly the same as given in Section 52 of the Pakistan Penal Code which says :

"Nothing is said to be done or believed in good faith which is done or believed without due care and attention."

Such a mistake is a good defence in *Ḥadd* cases. For example, if a person has sexual intercourse with a woman mistaking her as his wife, he cannot be punished for adultery. Or if a person sees something at a distance and, mistaking it as a prey, throws a missile at it and kills it, but later finds that it was a man, he is not liable to *Qiṣāṣ*.

But mistake is no excuse in cases of *ḥuqūq al-'ibād*. For example, if a person damages or destroys the property of another person by mistake, he is liable to pay compensation to the owner of it. Likewise, in the case of homicide mentioned above, blood-money is payable.

On the civil side, it has been said that if a person pronounces the divorce formula by mistake, the divorce becomes effective, according to the Ḥanafī jurists. But Shāfiʿī disagrees.

According to British jurisprudence as well, a mistake of fact is a good excuse. Section 79 of the Pakistan Penal Code says :

"Nothing is an offence which is done by any person who is justified by law, or who by reason of a mistake of fact and not by reason of a mistake of law in good faith, believes himself to be justified by law, in doing it."

On the civil side, a reference may be made to Section 20 of the Pakistan Contract Act which says :

" Where both the parties to an agreement are under a mistake as to a matter of fact essential to the agreement, the agreement is void."

But a unilateral mistake does not avoid a contract according to Section 22 of the said Act, which says :

" A contract is not voidable merely because it was caused by one of the parties to it being under a mistake as to a matter of fact.'

As a reason of this rule of law, it is said that "He had no right to make such a mistake."

But can it not be said with equal force that "They had no right to make such a mistake"?

(*xiii*) *Coercion*. The word used in *ikrāh* which means constraint or coercion. In Muslim Law, the word is defined as a compulsion, exercised by a person or brought about by circumstances under which he is forced to do or say something which he does not intend or like to do or say. The word has been defined in Section 15 of the Contract Act as follows :

"Coercion is the committing, or threatening to commit, any act forbidden by the Pakistan Penal Code, or the unlawful detaining, or threatening to detain, any property, to the prejudice of any person whatever, with the intention of causing any person to enter into an agreement."

Acts done under compulsion or coercion are of three kinds.

(*i*) Acts which are a duty and must be performed. The Qur'ān says :

حُرِّمَتْ عَلَيْكُمُ الْمَيْتَةُ وَالدَّمُ وَلَحْمُ الْخِنْزِيرِ...
فَمَنِ اضْطُرَّ فِي مَخْمَصَةٍ غَيْرَ مُتَجَانِفٍ لِإِثْمٍ فَإِنَّ اللَّهَ
غَفُورٌ رَحِيمٌ.

[" You are forbidden to eat that which dies of itself and blood and flesh of swine. . . . But whoever is compelled by hunger (to eat of what We have forbidden), not inclining wilfully to sin, then surely God is Forgiving, Merciful" (v. 3).]

Now, suppose that a person is extremely hungry and it is feared that he may die of starvation if he does not get anything to eat. Nothing but forbidden flesh is available. The Qur'ān permits him to eat it. Our jurists go further and say that under these circumstances, it is his duty to eat the forbidden flesh and he must eat it or he will be guilty of the sin of suicide.

According to a tradition given in the *Muwaṭṭā*, even an under-fed person, if he steals something to eat, would not be punished. The tradition says :

"The slaves of Ḥāṭib stole a camel belonging to a person of the Muzainah tribe and slaughtered and ate it. When the case came to 'Umar, he ordered that the hands of the slaves be cut off. But after a moment 'Umar said to Ḥāṭib, 'I think that you have been keeping your slaves hungry. By God, I will order you to pay such a heavy compensation, that you will feel the burden of it.' Then 'Umar asked the owner the price of the camel. He replied that he had refused to sell it at 400 dirhams a few days back. 'Umar then ordered Ḥāṭib to pay 800 dirhams to the owner of the camel."

(*ii*) Acts which are forbidden and should not be done even under compulsion of whatever kind it may be, e.g. adultery or murder.

It is submitted that this proposition of law as far as it relates to adultery cannot apply to women. A woman submitting to adultery under compulsion would not be guilty of any offence. The Qur'ān says:

وَلَا تُكْرِهُوا فَتَيَاتِكُمْ عَلَى الْبِغَاءِ إِنْ أَرَدْنَ تَحَصُّنًا لِّتَبْتَغُوا عَرَضَ
الْحَيَوٰةِ الدُّنْيَا ۚ وَمَن يُكْرِههُّنَّ فَإِنَّ اللَّهَ مِن بَعْدِ إِكْرَاهِهِنَّ
غَفُورٌ رَّحِيمٌ

["And compel not your slave-girls to prostitution when they desire to keep chaste, in order to seek the frail goods of this world's life. And whoever compels them, then surely after their compulsion Allah is Forgiving, Merciful" (xxiv. 33).]

There is a difference of opinion among our jurists on the question of liability of the person exercising coercion and of the person coerced, in such cases. According to Abū Ḥanīfah, the person exercising coercion is liable to *Qiṣāṣ* in case of a murder by the person coerced, because the former is the real murderer and the latter is just a tool in his hand. Muḥammad and Zufar say that the person coerced is liable to *Qiṣāṣ*, because he is the actual murderer. In the opinion of Shāfi'ī, both are liable to *Qiṣāṣ*, while, according to Abū Yūsuf, none of them is, because the case is doubtful.

This aspect of law, under British jurisprudence, is given in Sec. 94 of the Pakistan Penal Code, which says :

"Except murder, and offences against the State punishable with death, nothing is an offence which is done by a person who is compelled to do it by threats, which, at the time of doing it, reasonably cause the apprehension that instant death to that person will otherwise be the consequence : provided the person doing the act did not of his own accord, or from a reasonable apprehension of harm to himself short of instant death, place himself in the situation by which he became subject to such constraint."

(*iii*) Acts which a person under compulsion may or may not do as he chooses. For example, if a person is coerced by someone or compelled by circumstances to break his fast, it would be lawful for him to do so.

Another illustration of this proposition of law is given in the Qur'ān itself :

مَنْ كَفَرَ بِاللّٰهِ مِنْ بَعْدِ إِيمَانِهِ إِلَّا مَنْ أُكْرِهَ وَقَلْبُهُ مُطْمَئِنٌّ
بِالْإِيمَانِ وَلٰكِنْ مَنْ شَرَحَ بِالْكُفْرِ صَدْرًا فَعَلَيْهِمْ غَضَبٌ
مِنَ اللّٰهِ وَلَهُمْ عَذَابٌ عَظِيمٌ

["Whoso disbelieves in God after having believed (in Him), save him who is forced thereto, while his heart is content with faith, but he who opens (his) breast for disbelief, on them is the wrath of God and for them is a grievous chastisement" (xvi. 106).]

This verse relates to apostasy. Renunciation of Islam is, of course, the greatest of all the great sins. It is also an offence punishable with death, according to the majority of our jurists. The Qur'ān says that on apostates is wrath of Allah and theirs will be an awful doom. But it makes an exception for one who abandons Islam (by word of mouth) under coercion. In the early history of Islam we find instances of those who took advantage of this exception and of those who refused to do so and preferred torture and death to saying a word of disbelief.

On the civil side, according to the Ḥanafī school of law, if a person marries a woman under coercion or divorces her under coercion, the marriage or the divorce would be effective. As regards sales, it has been said that a sale made under coercion is not void though it is invalid and, therefore, if the person coerced agrees to the sale after coercion has ceased, the sale is validated and takes effect from the time it was made.

According to Shafi'ī', Mālikī and Ḥanbalī schools, a divorce pronounced by a person under compulsion is ineffective.

The following *ḥadīth* given in the *Bulūgh al-Marām* of Ibn Ḥajar 'Asqalānī covers the case of mistake, forgetfulness and coercion :

قال النبی صلی الله علیه وسلم ان الله تعالی وضع عن امتی الخطاء و النسیان وما استکرهوا علیه -

["The Prophet said : God has lifted away from my people the responsibility for acts done by mistake. in forgetfulness and under coercion."]

Section 19 of the Contract Act says :

"When consent to an agreement is caused by coercion . . . the agreement is a contract voidable at the option of the party whose consent was so Caused."

Before concluding, it may be noted that Muslim

jurisprudence mentions several other factors as well which effect *ahlīyyat*, but as they relate only to mat ters of faith and worship, they have been omittec here.

Chapter 4

EVOLUTION OF MUSLIM LAW

Background. Before the advent of Islam in Arabia, the country was inhabited mainly by the Sabians and partly by the Jews, the Christians and the Magians. Practically the religion of the whole of the Arab nation in that state of ignorance, the *jāhilī*, was chiefly gross idolatry. All these *jāhilī* religions are mentioned in the Holy Qur'ān :

إِنَّ الَّذِينَ آمَنُوا وَالَّذِينَ هَادُوا وَالصَّابِئِينَ وَالنَّصَارَىٰ
وَالْمَجُوسَ وَالَّذِينَ أَشْرَكُوا ۖ إِنَّ اللَّهَ يَفْصِلُ بَيْنَهُمْ
يَوْمَ الْقِيَامَةِ ۚ إِنَّ اللَّهَ عَلَىٰ كُلِّ شَيْءٍ شَهِيدٌ

["As to the true believers, and they who Judaise, and the Sabians, and the Christians, and the Magians and those who do idolatry : verily God shall judge between them on the Day of Resurrection; for God is witness of all things" (xxii. 17).]

Now, apart from those idolaters who were not known to be the followers of any prophet, the Jews and the Christians were followers of prophets and had their revealed books, the Old and the New Testaments, with them. The Sabians and the Magians are also generally believed to be the followers of true prophets of God and to possess scriptures. All these peoples had their laws, God-given and otherwise.

But about eighty per cent of the laws of a people are their customary laws or codified laws, based on custom. Naturally the Arabs, as well, had their customary laws, which they followed.

Is Islamic Law a purely New Law? Therefore, the question arises, whether Islamic law is a purely new law or is an improvement on the old Arab laws, divine and customary.

My reply to this question would be that the Muslim Law is an improvement on the old existing laws of the people of Arabia, and is, in no sense, totally new law. I base this assertion on our Holy Book itself.

It has been repeatedly stated in the Qur'ān that this book verifies the old revealed books, already with the people. This shows that the Qur'ān did not repeal the old existing Divine laws. It did, of course, improve upon those laws here and there. The Qur'ān says :

إِنَّ هَٰذَا لَفِي الصُّحُفِ الْأُولَىٰ ﴿١٨﴾ صُحُفِ إِبْرَاهِيمَ وَمُوسَىٰ

["Certainly this is in the earlier scriptures, the scriptures of Abraham and Moses" (xix. 87).]

No one can deny that much has been added to the old books by human hands, and it may be that some of their verses were lost and some altered as well. But it is a fact that the bulk of the God-given laws is still there in the Bible.

Much of the Muslim Law as given in the Qur'ān and in the Traditions of the Prophet is identically the same as at present found in the two Testaments.

Just a few examples would be sufficient to illustrate this proposition. In sūrah iv., verses 22 and 23, the Qur'ān gives the prohibited circle for marriage, on grounds of consanguinity and affinity. Compare this with the prohibited list as given in the third book of Moses "Leviticus," chapter 18, verses 6 to 18, and you will find that the Quranic list is just an improvement on the Biblical list. It, in no sense, repeals it. Prohibition on the ground of fosterage is not there in the Bible. The Qur'ān has mentioned it. The well-known passage from "Exodus," chapter 22, verses 23 and 24 "Life for life, eye for eye, tooth for tooth, hand for hand, foot for foot," etc., has been repeated in the Qur'ān :

وَكَتَبْنَا عَلَيْهِمْ فِيهَآ أَنَّ النَّفْسَ بِالنَّفْسِ وَ
الْعَيْنَ بِالْعَيْنِ وَالْأَنْفَ بِالْأَنْفِ وَ الْأُذُنَ بِالْأُذُنِ وَ
السِّنَّ بِالسِّنِّ وَالْجُرُوحَ قِصَاصٌ فَمَنْ تَصَدَّقَ بِهٖ فَهُوَ
كَفَّارَةٌ لَّهٗ

["And We prescribed to them in it that life is for life, and eye for eye, and nose for nose, and ear for ear, and tooth for tooth and (that there is) reprisal in wounds but he who forgoes it, it shall be expiation for him" (v. 45).]

The improvement made by the Qur'ān in this case, as well as in the case of all criminal offences, is that pardon has also been provided for. The law of crimes as given in the Old Testament does not recognise forgiveness anywhere. On the other hand, it says :

"And thine eye shall not pity; but life shall go for life, eye for eye, tooth for tooth, hand for hand, foot for foot" (Deuteronomy, chapter 19, verse 21).

Yes another example. The Qur'ān says .

يٰٓاَيُّهَا الَّذِيْنَ اٰمَنُوْا لَا تَقْرَبُوا الصَّلٰوةَ وَ اَنْتُمْ
سُكٰرٰى حَتّٰى تَعْلَمُوْا مَا تَقُوْلُوْنَ

["O you who believe! do not go near prayer when you are intoxicated until you know what you say" (iv. 43).]

The Bible says :

"Do not drink wine nor strong drink, thou, nor thy sons with thee, when you go into the tabernacle of the congregation, lest ye die : it shall be a statute for ever throughout your generations" (Leviticus, chapter 10, verse 9).

As regards the customary laws of a people, Islam definitely recognises them as long as they do not offend against the letter or the spirit of the Qur'ān or the *Sunnah*. The force behind the rules of custom is the common sense and the good conscience of a people. The Qur'ān says :

وَالْمُؤْمِنُوْنَ وَالْمُؤْمِنٰتُ بَعْضُهُمْ اَوْلِيَآءُ بَعْضٍ
يَأْمُرُوْنَ بِالْمَعْرُوْفِ وَيَنْهَوْنَ عَنِ الْمُنْكَرِ

["And the believing men and the believing women are guardians of each other; they enjoin good and forbid evil" (ix. 71).]

The words *ma'rūf* and *munkar* are usually taken to mean "good" and "evil" as here. But the word *ma'rūf* literally means something known and recognised and the word *munkar* means its opposite, something not known and not recognised. Therefore *ma'rūf* means something which people generally know and recognise and which they generally say and do. *Munkar* is just the opposite of it. For instance, people go out fully dressed, and they generally abstain from going out naked or half naked. Therefore to go out fully dressed is *ma'rūf* and to go out naked or half naked is *munkar*. The Qur'ān has thus recognised the enforceability of customary laws. As a matter of fact, the binding force of a rule of custom is as great as that of the *Ijmā'al Ummah*. The Ḥanafī jurists are unanimous on the proposition that a rule of customary law has a greater force than a rule of law deduced by the process of *Qiyās.*

It can, therefore, be safely stated that all the customary laws of *jāhilī* Arabia and later of other countries as well, excepting the laws that were specifically repealed or amended by the Qur'ān or the *Ḥadīth* became part and parcel of Islamic Laws, by adoption and adaption.

Now, the Biblical laws and the rules of the customary laws of Arabia and other countries which the Muslims conquered, were, so to say, the raw material from which the most beautiful and magnificent structure of Islamic Laws was constructed.

The First Period in the History of the Evolution of the Islamic Law. It would be conducive to better understanding if we divide the history of the evolution of Muslim Law into different periods. The first period began with the beginning of the revelation of the Qur'ān. It was a period of more than twenty-two years beginning from the forty-first year of the Prophet's life.

From time to time, during this period, several rules of the Civil, the Criminal, the Revenue, the International and the Constitutional Law were revealed. It may be noted here that, unlike the books of Moses, the Qur'ān was not profuse at all in this respect. The Book was not meant to be a code of law, exhaustive in any sense. As a matter of fact, many of the rules of law given in the Qur'ān were revealed in answer to the questions put by people. For example:

يَسْـَٔلُونَكَ عَنِ الْأَهِلَّةِ

["They ask thee about the new moons" (ii. 189).]

يَسْئَلُونَكَ مَاذَا يُنْفِقُونَ ط

["They ask thee what they should spend" (ii. 215).]

يَسْئَلُونَكَ عَنِ الشَّهْرِ الْحَرَامِ

["They ask thee concerning the sacred month" (ii. 217).]

يَسْئَلُونَكَ عَنِ الْخَمْرِ وَالْمَيْسِرِ ط

["They ask thee about intoxicants and games of chance" (ii. 219).]

يَسْئَلُونَكَ مَاذَا أُحِلَّ لَهُمْ ط

["They ask thee what is allowed to them" (v. 4).]

يَسْئَلُونَكَ عَنِ الْأَنْفَالِ ط

["They ask thee about the accessions" (viii. 1).]

وَيَسْئَلُونَكَ عَنِ الْيَتٰمٰى ط

["They ask thee concerning the orphans" (ii. 220).]

These are just a few instances out of a large number of such questions mentioned in the Holy Qur'ān.

As a matter of fact, God did not like these questions at all. He actually wanted to leave much of law to be made by man himself guided by his common sense and good conscience. The Qua'ān says:

أَمْ تُرِيدُونَ أَنْ تَسْئَلُوا رَسُولَكُمْ كَمَا سُئِلَ مُوسٰى
مِنْ قَبْلُ ط

["Is it that you wish to put questions to your Apostle, as Moses was questioned before?" (ii. 108).]

Again :

يٰاَيُّهَا الَّذِيْنَ اٰمَنُوْا لَا تَسْـَٔلُوْا عَنْ اَشْيَآءَ اِنْ تُبْدَ لَكُمْ تَسُؤْكُمْ
وَاِنْ تَسْـَٔلُوْا عَنْهَا حِيْنَ يُنَزَّلُ الْقُرْاٰنُ تُبْدَ لَكُمْ عَفَا اللّٰهُ
عَنْهَا وَاللّٰهُ غَفُوْرٌ حَلِيْمٌ ۝ قَدْ سَاَلَهَا قَوْمٌ مِّنْ قَبْلِكُمْ ثُمَّ اَصْبَحُوْا بِهَا
كٰفِرِيْنَ ۝

["O you who believe ! do not put questions about things which if declared to you may trouble you, and if you question about them when the Qur'ān is being revealed, they shall be declared to you. God pardons these, and God is Forbearing. A people before you indeed asked such questions, and then ceased to obey what was told them" (v. 101, 102).]

The Prophet, as well, expressed his dislike for such questions. Once he was asked if *Ḥajj* was to be performed every year. He replied: "If I had said yes to this question, *Ḥajj* would have become *farḍ* every year. As long as I leave you alone, leave me alone, because people before you met destruction on account of their manifold questions and their consequent disobedience." On another occasion he is reported to have said: "The greatest criminal among Muslims is he who asked a question about something which was not made unlawful for Muslims, but which was declared unlawful in reply to his question. God has imposed certain duties upon you. Do them. He has fixed some limits. Do not exceed them. Certain things have been declared by Him as invalid. Do not validate them. He has kept quiet over other things not because He has forgotten them but because He wants to be lenient to you. Therefore don't make searching inquiries about them."

I hope the reader would excuse me if I give a concrete example of it as I understand it. This relates to "they ask thee about intoxicants" (ii. 219). The Old and New Testaments are full of references to wine and other intoxicants. At places drinking of wine is declared undesirable and unworthy. At places its use is actually prescribed. At several places it is mentioned as one of God's gifts. Several Prophets, for instance Noah, Isaac, Jacob, Lot, David, Daniel and Christ and others are stated to have been drinking wine. Actually there are innumerable references to wine, for and against, in the Bible, but nowhere is its total prohibition mentioned.

Now the Qur'ān mentions intoxicants at four places :

وَمِنْ ثَمَرٰتِ النَّخِيْلِ وَالْاَعْنَابِ تَتَّخِذُوْنَ مِنْهُ سَكَرًا وَّ
رِزْقًا حَسَنًا

["And of the fruits of the palms and the grapes you obtain from them intoxication and goodly provision" (xvi. 67).]

Similar verses appear in the Bible at many places.

يَسْئَلُوْنَكَ عَنِ الْخَمْرِ وَالْمَيْسِرِ قُلْ فِيْهِمَآ اِثْمٌ كَبِيْرٌ
وَّمَنَافِعُ لِلنَّاسِ وَاِثْمُهُمَآ اَكْبَرُ مِنْ نَّفْعِهِمَا

["They ask thee about intoxicants and games of chance. Say: In both of them is great sin and some advantages for men, and their sin is greater than their advantages" (ii. 219).]

As has already been stated, the Bible is full of things like this.

يٰٓاَيُّهَا الَّذِيْنَ اٰمَنُوْا لَا تَقْرَبُوا الصَّلٰوةَ

["O ye who believe ! approach not prayers . . ." (iv. 43).]

This verse and its equivalent in the Bible have already been quoted. The Bible contains several verses of this nature.

يَاأَيُّهَا الَّذِينَ آمَنُوا إِنَّمَا الْخَمْرُ وَالْمَيْسِرُ وَالْأَنْصَابُ وَالْأَزْلَامُ
رِجْسٌ مِنْ عَمَلِ الشَّيْطَنِ فَاجْتَنِبُوهُ لَعَلَّكُمْ تُفْلِحُونَ ۝ إِنَّمَا
يُرِيدُ الشَّيْطَنُ أَنْ يُوقِعَ بَيْنَكُمُ الْعَدَاوَةَ وَالْبَغْضَاءَ فِي الْخَمْرِ
وَالْمَيْسِرِ وَيَصُدَّكُمْ عَنْ ذِكْرِ اللهِ وَعَنِ الصَّلٰوةِ فَهَلْ أَنْتُمْ مُنْتَهُونَ ۝

["O you who believe ! intoxicants and games of chance and (sacrificing to) stones set up and the (divining) arrows are only an uncleanness, the devil's work: shun it therefore that you may be successful. The devil only desires to cause enmity and hatred to spring in your midst by means of intoxicants and games of chance, and to keep you off from the remembrance of God and from prayer; will you then desist?" (v. 90-91).]

These two verses, after all, made the drinking of intoxicants *ḥarām*. The first three verses did not order total prohibition.

Now there is direct evidence to show that after the verse iv. 43 was revealed, people asked الهم بين لنا فى الخمر بيانا شافيا ["Our Lord! give us some clear and decisive order about *khamr*"]. The clear and decisive order came because we asked for it. But, in spite of the order, we drink and prove the truth of the saying of the Prophet that "people before you met destruction on account of their too many questions followed by disobedience."

That God and the Prophet did not want to give many laws has a clear proof in the fact that there is not much of law in the Qur'ān nor in the *Ḥadīth*. Out of hundreds of criminal offences only five or six have been dealt with in the Holy Book. On the civil side as well just a few pinciples of law relating to marriage, dower, divorce and inheritance, etc., are given in the Qur'ān. The same is the case of *Ḥadīth*.

What law the Prophet gave in this period relates

to the questions of details which arose in particular and specific cases which came up for decision before him.

The first period of the evolution of Islamic Law came to an end at the death of the Prophet on 12 Rabīʿ al-Awwal in the eleventh year of the Hijri era.

The Second Period. The second period in the history of evolution of Islamic Laws dated from 11 A.H. and it lasted for about a century. During this period, the work of law-giving or law-making remained throughout in the hands of the Companions. State service, trade and travel had taken a large number of the Companions of the Prophet to different countries conquered by Muslims during this period. Whenever and wherever a law point which was not directly covered by the Holy Book came up for decision. The people naturally referred it to the Companions. As a matter of fact they acted as legislators, jurists and judges throughout this century. They had seen the Prophet deciding law cases and they had heard him saying things. They were, therefore, the repositories of the *Sunnah*, the second best source of Muslim law. Primarily they were only exponents of the *Sunnah*. But as each case had its own peculiar facts, the Companions every now and then faced new points of law and had to decide them. They were, therefore, actually making new law as well all the time. Of course, they did everything in this connection in the light of the *Kitāb* and the *Sunnah*. But difficulties arose.

Unlike the Qur'ān, the *Ḥadīth* had not been compiled in book form. It has been stated that one or two of the Companions had with them their brief collections of *Ḥadīth* reduced into writing. But this statement is not free from doubt. Man is man after all and not very long after the death of the Prophet the Muslims came face to face with a difficult problem : "How to distinguish a true *ḥadīth* from a forged one ?" Abū Bakr is reported to have collected people and told them : "You narrate *aḥādīth* to people and you differ between yourselves regarding these traditions. People who will come after you shall differ still more. Therefore you should not relate any *ḥadīth*. If anybody asks you a question, tell him that the Qur'ān is with us. What is *ḥarām* according to it is *ḥarām* and what is *ḥalāl* according to it is *ḥalāl*." Somebody asked Abū Hurairah if he used to narrate as many traditions in the time of 'Umar as he did at that time. Abū Hurairah replied : "If I had done so in the time of 'Umar, he would have whipped me."

It is impossible to believe that Abū Bakr and 'Umar would have taken up this attitude towards *Sunnah*, the most valuable source after the Qur'ān, if "false coins" had not been inseparably mixed up with this treasure.

Anyhow, the Companions were busy giving law to the Muslims in different cities of the Muslim world of that period. They always followed the *Kitāb* and the *Sunnah* in all cases covered by these sources in letter or in spirit. Some of the more renowned Companions of the Prophet and some others who were responsible for the evolution of Muslim Law during this period may be briefly mentioned here.

(1) *Khulafā'i Rāshidīn*. They were the heads of the Muslim State, one after the other. They were admin-

istrators, law-givers and judges. A *Qāḍī* for deciding law cases was for the first time appointed by 'Umar. The first Caliph had already erected jails for the custody of criminals. This was the first attempt at methodical administration of justice which later developed into a regular system in this century.

The Caliphs usually accepted a *ḥadīth* only if its genuineness was proved by direct evidence. They never acted on the statement of one man only.

(2) *'Ā'ishah.* She was considered to be the biggest Muslim jurist of her time. She was naturally the most dependable authority on *Sunnah.* She died in the year 57/676.

(3) *'Abd Allah b. 'Umar.* He was a son of the second Caliph. He embraced Islam while he was a minor. He is known to be a good narrator of *ḥadīth* but not a very good jurist. He used to give *fatwās* at the *Ḥajj* congregations. He died in the year 73/692.

(4) *Abū Hurairah.* Out of the Companions of the Prophet he remembered and narrated the largest number of *aḥādīth.* He was a great *nuftī* of his time. He died in the year 58/678.

(5) *'Abd Allah b. 'Abbās.* He was born two years before *Hijrah* and died in 68/687. It is believed that the knowledge of the people of Mecca in *Ṭafsīr* and law was wholly based upon what they learnt from him.

(6) *'Alqamah b. Qais,* died 62/682.

(7) *'Ubaidah b. 'Umar al-Salmānī,* died 92/711.

(8) *Shuraiḥ b. al-Ḥārith.* He was appointed *Qāḍī* at Kufah by the second Caliph. He worked in that capacity for sixty-three years and died in 78/697.

(9) *Anas b. Mālik.* He remained in the service of

the Prophet for eleven years. A large number of *aḥādīth* have come down to us through him. He died in 93/712.

(10) *'Abd al-Raḥmān b. Ghanam al-Ash'arī*. He was sent to Syria by the second Caliph, to teach *Fiqh* to people there. He died in 78/697.

(11) *'Abd Allah b. 'Amr b. al-'Āṣ*. He is stated to have written down what he had heard from the Prophet. He died in 65/684.

It may be noted here that no attempt at codification of Muslim Law was made during this period. Whenever a new point of law arose, it was decided by the *Muftīs* and *Qāḍīs* of the place.

For the first half of this period the exposition of law and law-giving remained mainly in the hands of the Companions of the Prophet, but in the second half this work was mainly in the hands of the successors to the Companions (*Tābi'īn*) of the Prophet.

During all this period the Companions and the successors were posted in different cities all over the Muslim Empire of the time. Naturally, therefore, some of the customary law of the different provinces of the Empire was gradually incorporated in Muslim Laws. It has been suggested that some points of the Roman Law were, as well, adopted.

The Third Period. And now we come to the third period in this history. This is the period in which the four *Imāms* of Muslim jurisprudence lived and worked. The Companions had all died during the last period. Some of the Successors were, of course, alive in the earlier part of this third period as well.

Roughly speaking, this period covered the second and the first half of the third century of the Hijri era.

Imām-i A'ẓam, viz. Imām Abū Ḥanīfah, lived from 80/699 to 150/767, Imām Mālik from 93/712 to 179/795, Imām Shāfi'ī from 150/767 to 204/719 and Imām Aḥmad b. Ḥanbal from 164/778 to 241/855. The four *Imāms* founded the four different schools of Muslim jurisprudence, known as the *Madhāhib-i Arba'ah*, the Ḥanafī, the Mālikī, the Shāfi'ī and the Ḥanbalī schools.

It may be noted here that, in spite of the difference of opinion on so many law points, all the four *madhāhibs* are recognised to be the true *madhāhibs* by the followers of each and every one of them. Accordingly a *Qāḍī* of one *madhhib* is permitted to decide a case according to any one of the other three *madhāhibs*, if it is desirable under the particular circumstances of that case.

A large majority of the Muslims of the world are followers of the Ḥanafī school. It is followed in Turkey, the countries of old Turkish Empire, Central Asia, India and Pakistan. The Shāfi'ī school is followed in Egypt, South Arabia, the Indian Archipelago, East Africa and Syria. The Mālikī school is followed in the Maghrib, Upper Egypt and parts of West Africa. The Ḥanbalī school is now limited to Najd only.

The work of the codification of Muslim Law on scientific lines was taken in hand during the period under consideration. The very first attempt in this line was the *Muwaṭṭā* of Imām Mālik. This work represents a codification of the *Fiqh* as it developed in the Hijaz in its theological centre, Medina. Almost at the same time, Muslim Law was being methodically systematised in other parts of the Muslim

Empire also. The two well-known disciples of Imām Abū Ḥanīfāh, viz. Imām Abū Yūsuf and Imām Muḥammad, wrote books on Muslim Law, followed by others.

This was the period of *Ijtihād*. As has already been stated, the *Kitāb* and the *Sunnah* had left much law to be made by the Muslims themselves. Consequently *Qiyās*, the third source of Muslim Law, was resorted to. This process of evolving law is the deductions from the Qur'ān and the *Sunnah* by reasoning by analogy. The expansion of the Empire, as well, raised questions previously unknown. Answers to these questions could not be found in the first two sources of law. People, therefore, found themselves forced to take decisions and to regulate their conduct from their own opinion. Imām Abū Ḥanīfah evolved another process as well. This is known as *Istiḥsān*. This is the name given to a method of argument to settle *Fiqh* rules in conformity with the requirements of everyday life, equity or social conditions. A similar process was adopted by Imām Mālik which is known as *Istiṣlāḥ*. According to both these methods, the results of *Qiyās* are often simply disregarded when it is considered necessary or simply desirable to depart from the strict demands of theory. It is therefore that both these methods are objected to by many and have never been generally recognised as reliable fundamentals in the science of law.

Of the four *Imāms*, Imām-i A'ẓam was the greatest advocate of free thinking and independent opinion. But there were also people who would not agree to recognise the opinion of any mortal (excepting of course the Prophet) as a deciding factor in legislation. It was not conceivable, they said, that the *Kitāb* and the *Sunnah* had left anything undetermined. They believed that all the contingencies that might arise in the future were also provided for in these two sources of law. Consequently, the jurists became divided in two distinct groups, the *Aṣḥāb al-Ḥadīth* and the *Aṣḥāb al-Rā'i*.

We must remember that by the close of the Khilāfat-i Rāshidah Muslims were divided into three factions, the *Jamhūr*, the Shī'ah and the Khārijī. This was a political division, but it was bound to have its repercussions on Islamic Law. Consequently an incentive to the publication of false *aḥādīth* came into existence. Later other motives for forging traditions also came into action. The Zanādiqah were the worst criminals in this respect. Some unscrupulous people fabricated these traditions to please their rulers and other magnates. Still later the division of jurists into two sects, the *Aṣḥāb al-Rā'i* and the *Aṣḥāb al-Ḥadīth*, was also responsible for the publication of a very large number of false *aḥādīth*. Thus with the vast number of forged traditions it became possible to quote a *ḥadīth* on any point of law that arose under any contingency and readily to dispense with the necessity of *Rā'ī* and *Qiyās*.

It was under these difficult conditions that the Imām-i A'ẓam had to work. He subjected every tradition to a very critical scrutiny, with the result that it has been stated that he acted on only eighteen *aḥādīth* out of a very large number of such traditions which had been published during his time. The rest of his *Fiqh* was all based on the Qur'ān, *Qiyās* and *Rā'i*.

On the other hand, the Mālikī and the Ḥanbalī schools resorted to *Qiyās* and *Rā'i* very seldom. It is worthy of notice here that Imām Aḥmad b. Ḥanbal compiled a *Ḥadīth* collection containing fifty thousand traditions though some people say that this book was not written by the Imām, but has been wrongly attributed to him with a purpose.

Between the Mālikī and the Ḥanbalī schools on the one hand and the Ḥanafi school on the other Imām Shāfi'ī was a mediator.

It would be interesting to note here that the Ḥanafī school, being the most progressive and rational of the four schools, is followed by an overwhelming majority of the Muslims of the world, while the Ḥanbalī school, not being progressive at all, is followed by a very small number of people living in Najd, a province of Arabia.

The fourth source of Muslim Law, after *Kitāb*, *Sunnah* and *Qiyās*, is *Ijmā'*. Some authorities put *Ijmā'* before *Qiyās*. But the fact is that *Qiyās* is both before and after *Ijmā'*. *Ijmā'* means the agreement of jurists on a certain point of law. A section of our jurists limits the authority of *Ijmā'* to the consensus of opinion of the Companions of the Prophet. Some jurists include the agreement of the Successors as well in the definition of *Ijmā'*, but they do not go further. Imām-i A'ẓam recognises the authority of the *Ijmā'* of all times.

Consequently, the *Ijmā'* of the period now under consideration played an important part in the evolution of law, though Imām Aḥmad b. Ḥanbal and Imām Shāfi'ī refused to recognise the authority of it.

The Fourth Period. The fourth period of this history covered the second half of the third century and the fourth century of the Muslim era.

In the closing years of the last period and during this period the most authoritative and renowned six collections of *Ḥadīth* were compiled and published. They are known as *Ṣiḥāḥ Sittah*. The compilers were Bukhārī (d. 256/870), Muslim (d. 268/874), Abū Dāwūd (d. 275/888), Tirmidhī (d. 279/892) Nasā'ī (d. 303/915) and Ibn Mājah (d. 273/886).

The publication of the *Ṣiḥāḥ Sittah* had a great and far-reaching effect on *Fiqh*. Imām Bukhārī's book is unanimously considered the most truthful book after the Qur'ān. Bukhārī was very much against the *Fiqh* of Imām-i A'ẓam but the *Ṣaḥīḥ Bukhārī* is all the same respected by the Ḥanafī jurists as well. All the books of *Fiqh* written during this period contain copious references to the traditions given in the *Ṣāḥīḥ*. Although Imām-i A'ẓam himself, as has already been stated, admitted the truthfulness of only seventeen or eighteen *aḥādīth*, the standard books on law written by his followers rely on hundreds of such traditions taken from the *Ṣiḥāḥ*. Consequently, much change of view on many legal points, in the Ḥanafī school of jurisprudence, was the result.

Thus, all the *Ijtihād* (if it could be called *Ijtihād*) done by Muslim jurists after the publication of the *Ṣiḥāḥ Sittah* was mainly based on the traditions given in these six books. It can, therefore, be stated that these books were responsible for the evolution of Islamic Law throughout this period of our history. A fairly large number of books on Muslim Law were written during this time.

The Fifth Period. The fifth period in the history

of evolution of Islamic Law began with the fifth century of the Hijri era and has not come to an end so far. Even today we are living in that period. This is the period of *Taqlīd*. We were asked to follow what people of the past ages said and to follow with folded hands and closed eyes. Like good people we obeyed. It was dogmatically asserted that the door of *Qiyās* and *Rā'i* and *Ijtihād* was closed and locked once for all, in the fourth century. It was further stated that people of the past had actually decided all the law points which could possibly arise in the future. This intellectual slavery was imposed on us and we accepted it. No one who lived during this period was entitled to be called a *Mujtahid* and the fact is that no one even in the fourth century of our era could win the title of a real *Mujtahid*.

A very large number of books on Islamic Law were written during this period, but these books were mere compilations. One man wrote a small text-book on *Fiqh* based entirely on the opinions of the people of the past. Another man wrote marginal notes on that book. The third man attempted a commentary on the book and the fourth a commentary on the commentary and so on. Therefore almost all the books on Muslim Law that we have with us at the present time are mere attempts at compiling, arranging and rearranging the same old existing material. Nothing original based on independent thinking can be found in these books. The most recent and standard work on Islamic Law is the *Fatāwā'-i 'Ālamgīrī* written and published under the orders and supervision of Emperor Aurangzeb. From end to end of this book which is in several big volumes one does not come across a single item of independent opinion on any point of law.

There has been, therefore, no evolution of our law during all this long period. Everything has stood still for about ten centuries. We have ceased to think and to differ and it is a miracle that we yet live.

Now follows discussion on the possibility and the necessity of the reconstruction of our law and, in my opinion, it is high time that we take up that work seriously. Unless we do so there is no hope of our being ruled by our own laws at any time.

Chapter 5

THE RECONSTRUCTION OF MUSLIM LAW

By the grace of God, once again we are a free, independent and sovereign nation. This change of status has brought into prominence the important question, "What should be the constitution and the law of our land ?"

Since Partition, there has been a unanimous and persistent demand that Pakistan should now be governed by Muslim Law and the Pakistan Constitution should be the Muslim Constitution. So far we have been ruled by laws made by Englishmen and these laws, both on Civil and Criminal sides, have not much in common with laws given to us by the Qur'ān, the first and the basic source of all Muslim laws. They are actually poles asunder on some points. Just one instance will be sufficient to illustrate and prove this assertion. Suppose A marries B today. B gives birth to a baby tomorrow. This baby shall be deemed conclusively to be the legitimate child of A, under section 112 of the Indian Evidence Act as adapted by Pakistan.

That this demand of the Muslim public is genuine, well founded and legitimate goes without saying. But this question is very closely connected with another equally, if not more, important question: is Muslim Law in its present conditions, and as codified by our jurists, suitable for and acceptable by the present times and conditions? A fairly large portion of the intelligentsia of Pakistan would, in words or at least in heart, give a negative reply to this question. It would be idle and possibly dangerous to ignore this extremely important question and its far-reaching consequences. Something which comes before us may not be beautiful and attractive, but we cannot safely shut our eyes to it. Therefore, we have got to face this aspect of the matter with manliness and intelligence.

Should we, and could we, reconstruct the Muslim Law to suit our present requirements and conditions? I would say: Yes!

The orthodox section of our people would vehemently condemn this "yes". If their No prevails, Muslim Law will never become the law of our land. Eminently learned Muslims of our time have always and unanimously replied to this question in the affirmative. I was a school student when 'Allāmah Iqbāl came to Abbottabad and spoke in favour of the reconstruction of Muslim Law in a meeting held in the Municipal Garden. Since then I had been seeing Dr Iqbāl off and on, till some time before his death. He never changed his opinion in this matter. Once he wrote to Sayyid Sulaimān Nadwī on this subject, but he received a negative reply. This is an instance of what our men of learning think and feel in this matter.

In my opinion this question has never been seriously gone into in a logical and scientific way; and this is the reason why there is such a great divergence of opinion between men like Iqbāl and Sulaimān Nadwī.

Now, If we carefully analyse the sources of Muslim Law and deal with each one of them separately, scientifically and philosophically, this difference of opinion can be narrowed down immediately.

The sources of Muslim Law are as follows: (1) The Holy Qur'ān, (2) *Ḥadīth* or *Sunnah*, (3) *Ijmā' al-Ummah*, (4) *Qiyās*.

As regards the first source, the Qur'ān, it may be noted that the Holy Book does not claim to be an exhaustive code of law. But certain sections of Civil, Criminal and Revenue Law are definitely given in the Holy Book. The Qur'ān, it should be remembered, gives us universal immutable and eternal truths. No question, therefore, of altering or reconstructing the law given in the Qur'ān can possibly arise. Those who profess to be Muslims can under no circumstances think of any such thing in any sense. God-given law stands and it shall stand for ever. But the question of interpretation of the Quranic verses is different. Men in the past have been interpreting the *āyāt* according to their own lights and have differed from each other in their interpretation. It follows that the man of today and the man of tomorrow have also got an undeniable right to do the same. No man with a grain of common sense could tolerate the dictum that the door of interpretation, even, was closed long ago.

A section of the educated Muslims believe that certain penal laws given in the Holy Book are intolerably harsh, such as cutting off a man's hand for theft. If this punishment is brutal, how shall one describe the punishment in Hell detailed in the Qur'ān? The only straightforward and honest way out for such people is to denounce Islam and have done with it. But the fact is that a grave and serious misunderstanding is responsible for all this trouble. It is generally believed that all theft is punishable with ampu-tation. But this is not the case. L ke all other penal codes of the world, the Qur'ān always mentions the maximum punishment which can be awarded for an offence. Therefore only extreme cases of theft shall be punished with this extreme punishment. In other cases of theft other punishments may be awarded.

Unfortunately, even our jurists of old have not appreciated this aspect of law correctly. There is definite and direct evidence in the *Ḥadīth* that this punishment is the maximum punishment that can be awarded in a theft case, e.g. the Holy Prophet has said that there shall not be cutting of hand in the case of theft of less than a certain amount and there shall not be cutting of hand for a theft of this or that article or from such and such a place. The only conclusion that one can arrive at from these traditions is that cutting of hand is the maximum punishment for theft. On the other hand, curiously enough, our jurists with all their learning misconstrued these traditions to mean that the theft of an amount less than a certain amount, and the theft of such and such articles and the theft from such and such a place, etc., was no theft at all. Such thefts do not come under the very definition of theft as framed by our jurists.

Now, to say that even in hard and extremely dark cases of theft, cutting of hand is an unduly harsh punishment, is, to say the least, nothing but the false humanitarianism. Of course, the thieves and prospective thieves could, with good reason, say so. As a matter of fact, the law of crimes as given in the Qur'ān is the most lenient penal law in the world.

It should be remembered that the Holy Book mentions just a few, five or six, offences. Hundreds of other offences can freely be made the subject of legislation according to our present-day circumstances and requirements. The same is the case regarding civil laws.

Turning to the second source of Muslim Law, the *Ḥadīth*, it may be stated here that this is second in authority to the Holy Book. This source of law is of very great value to Muslim jurists and is an invaluable treasure of guiding principles of law. But it must be remembered that the Holy Prophet was a man and lived amongst men. He had to deal with all sorts of details in all sorts of individual legal cases. Therefore his pronouncements on particular details under individually particular circumstances could not possibly be given that finality and immutability which the Quranic dicta possess. For instance, if in a case he fixed a certain amount of money as fine or compensation for one thing or a standard for another, could that be the last word on that subject for us now after fourteen hundred years, in a different country and under totally different economical conditions ? Surely not. Take a concrete example. The Holy Prophet fixed the blood-money for culpable homicide at one thousand dīnārs or one hundred camels. Shall we take it as a fixed standard for all cases and for all times and under all sorts of economic conditions ? I would say, No.

Yet another example of it is the case of *Zakāt*. The payment of *Zakāt* is not an individual and private concern as we generally consider it. It is a State tax. The payment of *Zakāt* is one of the five pillars of Islam. Its payment has repeatedly and very forcefully been ordered by God. The word appears in the Qur'ān at no less than thirty places. There are numerous other references to it in the Holy Book though couched in other words. But because State necessities vary in different countries and at different times the Qur'ān has nowhere fixed the amount to be paid as *Zakāt*. The Holy Prophet fixed a proportion (2½%) for his country and for his time. Compare the economic conditions prevailing in Arabia at that time and the amount of money required for State affairs in those days with the conditions of Pakistan today. Can you honestly say that the proportion fixed by the Holy Prophet at that time is binding on the State in these days? Certainly not. Though the general and universal principles do not change, the details do change with the change of time and circumstances.

But it should be remembered always that those principles of law given in the *Ḥadīth*, which are of general applicability, shall stand as they are for all times.

Apart from this, a thorough and scientific scrutiny of a *ḥadīth* is extremely necessary before we could take it as an authority for any law point. It cannot be denied that a fairly large number of such traditions have been included in the *Ḥadīth* collections as you would never accept as true. It would be perfectly useless to say that people of old have done this scrutiny and that we are bound to accept their conclusions as correct with folded hands and closed eyes. Nobody would agree to do so today and therefore we have got to face facts.

As an example, take this *ḥadīth*. It is said that "a person accused of theft was brought before the Holy Prophet. He ordered that his hand be cut off. It was done. The man committed theft again and the Prophet ordered that his foot be cut off. It was cut off. He committed theft for the third time. The Holy Prophet ordered that his second hand be cut off and so was done. He again committed theft and the Prophet ordered that his second foot be amputated. This was done. The man (with no hands and no feet) committed theft for the fifth time. The Holy Prophet ordered that he should be killed. He was killed accordingly and dragged to a well and thrown down in it and then a volley of stones was hurled at him." Would you believe that this fantastic story is a true *ḥadīth*? And yet it appears in the collections of Abū Dāwūd and Nasā'ī, two of the six most renowned books of *Ḥadīth*, the *Ṣiḥāḥ Sittah*. It is also there in the *Sharḥ al-Sunnah*.

The third source of Muslim Law and naturally the third in authority is the *Ijmā' al-Ummah*. It means the agreement of the *Mujtahids* of the Muslim people (i.e. those who have a right, in virtue of knowledge, to form a judgment of their own), in any age, on any matter of the faith. *Ijmā'* could be expressed in speech (*Ijmā' al-Qawl*) or in action (*Ijmā' al-Fi'l*) or by silence regarded as assent (*Ijmā' al-Sukūt*). It is especially excluded that it means the agreement of masses. Briefly stated *Ījmā'* means the consensus of opinion of our jurists on any point of law.

We know that the Qur'ān determines just a few principles and points of Civil, Criminal and Revenue Law. The *Ḥadīth*, as well, covers only a limited section of these laws. So, about 80 to 90% of our laws are those which are based on the opinion of our *Mujtahids* and jurists. It follows, therefore, that this portion of our laws is open to reconstruction in the light of the present-day conditions, without the least objection. But objections to this statement also would be coming forth with equal vehemence. The reason is that a fairly big section of our jurists have decreed that the door to *Ijtihād* and free thinking was closed and locked by Providence in the fourth century of the Hijri era, and that there was nothing left for people who came later but to follow and follow blindly. I hope that such pious dicta based on the worship of the past could not be swallowed by any sensible man living today. There is absolutely no logic in saying : "Well, we found our forefathers saying this or doing that." This worship of the past is one of the greatest obstacles in the progress of a nation. Muslims all over the world have suffered and are suffering a lot on account of this tendency. An Arabic poet says :

قل لمن لم يرالمعاصر شيئا   و يرى للاوائل التقديما

ان ذاک القديم کان حديثاً   و سيبقى هذا الحديث قديما

["Tell him who considers his contemporaries as of no worth and gives precedence to the people of the Past over the people of the Present, that the thing of the Past was the thing of the Present one day and the thing of the Present shall become the thing of the Past after some time."]

When the four greatest jurists of Islam, viz. the four *Imāms*, Imām Abū Ḥanīfah (b. 80/699), Imām Mālik (b. 93/712), Imām Shāfi'ī (b. 150/767) and Imām Aḥmad b. Ḥanbal (b. 164/781), thought over Muslim Law independently and differed from each other and actually founded four different schools of Muslim jurisprudence, they in fact practically demonstrated to the Muslim world that independent thinking and honest difference of opinion was a sign of life. Therefore to think of a fifth, a sixth and a seventh school of Muslim jurisprudcnce is no blasphemy.

It was one of the four *Imāms*, I do not exactly remember which, who, when somebody told him: "You say this, but so and so who were before you have said otherwise," replied: "What then 'They are men and we are men' (هم رجال و نحن رجال) signify ?"

To cease thinking independently and to cease differing is to die. And if we want to live, we shall have to think and to differ and bring our laws in conformity with the present-day conditions. If I can be excused for quoting Abū al-Faḍl, he said :

اگر امام اعظم در زمان ما مے بود فقہے دیگر مے نوشت

["If the great *Imām* [Imām Abū Ḥanīfah] had lived in our times, he would have written a different code of Law."]

The last source of Muslim Law is *Qiyās*. *Qiyās* means the deduction of legal propositions from the first three sources, by means of analogy. Here, again, it has been said that after the first three centuries of the Hijri era, nobody has a right even to resort to *Qiyās*.

If we give serious thought to this matter with an open and unprejudiced mind, we shall be convinced that reconstruction of Muslim Law is not only possible, but is, as well, a great necessity of the present times.

Chapter 6

IJTIHĀD

Ijtihād. Ijtihād is the exercise of one's opinion in the deduction of legal prescriptions from the Qur'ān, the *Ḥadīth* and the *Ijmā'* by way of *Qiyās* and *Istiḥsān*, etc., on points which are not definitely and directly determined by the first two sources of Muslim Law mentioned above. A jurist doing *Ijtihād* is called a *Mujtahid*.

The word *ijtihād* is derived from the root-word *jihd* which means : "striving, struggling, exerting oneself, care and diligence". It goes without saying, therefore, that it is the very first and foremost duty of a *Mujtahid* to do all that is in his power to come to a correct decision on the legal or theological point before him.

Taqlīd. It would not be out of place to define the word *taqlīd* as well, before we go further. *Taqlīd* means "to follow the opinion of a jurist, expressed in words or actions, without understanding or examining the reasons on which that opinion is based, on the presumption that he must have held that opinion for good reasons." Such a follower is called a *Muqallid*.

The word *taqlīd* comes from the root-word *qilādah* which means "a collar, necklace, chain, or any ornament for the neck ; a leash for holding a dog ; a term applied in enumerating elephants".

It may be noted here that, as follows from the above definition, a person who accepts the opinion of another person, after examining and agreeing with the reasons which form the basis of that opinion, is not a *Muqallid* in the true sense of the word. But we see that the jurists who belong to a particular school of Muslim Law and who, in most cases, follow the opinion of the older jurists of that school, though not blindly, are also called *Muqallids*. Thus a jurist who is a *Mujtahid* may at the same time be a *Muqallid* in this popular sense of the word. But keeping in view their correct and exact meanings, the two words *Mujtahid* and *Muqallid* are antonyms.

Qualifications for Ijtihād. According to Baghawī, a *Mujtahiḍ* should be master of the following five branches of learning: (*a*) knowledge of the Qur'ān including knowledge of the repealed and the repealing verses, (*b*) knowledge of the *Ḥadīth* relating to legal propositions, including the knowledge of different kinds of these traditions and the ability to reconcile a tradition with the Qur'ān when, on the face of it, it goes against the spirit or the letter of a Quranic verse, (*c*) knowledge of the opinions of the jurists of old on law points, their consensus and their differences, (*d*) knowledge of the Arabic language, and (*e*) knowledge of the methods of deduction of legal prescriptions from the Qur'ān and the *Ḥadīth* by way of *Qiyas*, i.e. by reasoning by analogy, including investigation of the *'illat al-Shara'*, i.e. the motive of law, the *ratio legis*. Moreover, a *Mujtahid* should be a devout, religious and pious person, but some jurists have said that this is not a necessary qualification for

Ijtihād. Ghazālī in his book on Muslim jurisprudence, the *Musṭaṣfā* says: "Piety of the *Mujtahid* is a condition precedent for the acceptance of the result of his *Ijtihād* and not for the correctness of it."

Some writers have gone too far in the matter of the necessary qualifications of a *Mujtahid.* For example, Aḥmad b. Ḥanbal is said to have expressed the opinioin that it is necessary for *Ijtihād* that the *Mujtahid* should have committed to memory at least half a million *aḥādīth.* This is on the face of it fantastic. It has also been said that the minimum qualification of a *Mujtahid* is that he should know by heart the whole of the *Mabsūṭ*, a large book on Muslim Law.

Different Kinds of Mujtahids. Shāh Walī Allah in his booklet the *'Iqd al-Jīd* mentions the following kinds of *Mujtahids*:

(1) *Mujtahid Muṭlaq*, i.e. a *Mujtahid* with a general, absolute and unlimited power of *Ijtihād*, e.g. Abū Ḥanīfah, Mālik, Shāfi'ī and Aḥmad b. Ḥanbal, the founders of the four schools of Muslim Law. All *Mujtahids* possessing the above-mentioned qualifications are of this kind. *Mujtahids Muṭlaq* are also of two kinds.

(*a*) *Mujtahid Mustaqil*, i.e. an independent *Mujtahid.* He can amend the rules which are the basic principles for the deduction of legal prescriptions. He may also put his own interpretation on the text of the original sources of Muslim Law, the *Kitāb* and *Sunnah*, and differ from the opinion of the jurists of old on any proposition of law. The above-named four *Imāms* belong to this class.

(*b*) *Mujtahid Muṭlaq Muntasib*, i.e. *Mujtahid* related or attached to a *Mujtahid Mustaqil*. He examines, understands and believes in the correctness and efficacy of the basic principles and rules framed by his master, the *Mujtahid Mustaqil*, to whom he is attached. He takes help from what his master has said, during his *Ijtihād*. He fully understands and appreciates the arguments of his master in favour of the legal propositions framed by him. He may, by the exercise of his *Ijtihād*, decide all new questions and points of law that come before him.

(2) *Mujtahid Fī al-Madhhab*. He belongs to a particular school of Muslim Law and follows the founder of that school in case of all legal propositions expressly determined by him. He knows the principles and the rules on which the *Imām* has based his system of jurisprudence. He does *Ijtihād* in case of new questions of law which have not been answered by his master, but he does so according to the rules framed by him.

(3) *Mujtahid Fī al-Fatwā*. He knows fully well his master's system of jurisprudence. If he finds two different statements of his master on a point of law, he can give one statement in preference to the other. In case of difference of opinion between the disciples of his master, he may prefer one opinion to the other.

It may be noted here that the above classification of the *Mujtahids* does not claim to be a strictly logical division, because there is much of overlapping in it.

Exercise of Free Opinion Advocated. In the early

history of Muslim jurisprudence, blind *Taqlīd* was unknown. The right of every person to differ from any other person was generally recognised. We know the story of an old woman who debated a law point with 'Umar the Great and won. Instances of a Companion differing from another Companion and a Successor (*Tabi'ī*) differing from a Companion can be found in great numbers. Ibn 'Abbās, one of the most learned Companions, differed on many law points from the older Companions who had gone before him. As related in *Al-Manār* and other books on Muslim jurisprudence, Shuraiḥ, the judge who was a Successor (*Tabi'ī*), differed from 'Alī on a point of the law of evidence. Masrūq, a Successor, differed from Ibn 'Abbās on a law point and his view was unanimously accepted.

Apart from this, most of our great scholars and jurists belonging to the early period of the history of Muslim Law have been advocating the exercise of free and independent opinion in matters of law and have been discouraging people from *Taqlīd*. Manṣūr, the 'Abbāsī Caliph, once suggested that copies of the books of Imām Mālik be sent to all the judges in the Empire, so that they may decide law cases according to them. Mālik prevented him from doing so saying that everybody should be left free to decide legal questions according to his own lights and no one should be forced to accept and act upon the opinion of another person.

Mu'ādh b. Jabal, 'Umar, 'Alī, Ibn 'Abbās and Ibn Mas'ūd used to say that no one should ask their opinion on any law point which had not actually arisen in a case, because, they said, during all times to come, there would be people who could decide these points whenever they arose.

According to the *'Iqd al-Jīd*, Abū Yūsuf, Zufar, and 'Āfiyah b. Zaid have said that no one should follow them in deciding a case unless he knows and fully understands the source of law which is the basis of their opinion. Abū Ḥanīfah also says: "It is not lawful for anyone to give *Fatwā* based on my opinion unless he understands my arguments in favour of that view." Aḥmad b. Ḥanbal says: "Do not follow me nor follow Mālik nor anyone else. Follow the Qur'ān and the *Ḥadīth* as they had done." Shāfi'ī has said: "The word of one man or even of a large number of men is not the last word on any point of law, excepting the word of the Prophet. Nor is the *Qiyās*, etc., of any person binding on any other person.

Ibn Ḥazm, who is an extremist in his views and often oversteps the bounds of moderation, goes much farther than everyone else and says that *Taqlīd* is absolutely *ḥarām* for everybody and under all circumstances.

Difference of Opinion, A Blessing. During the first three centuries of the Hijri era, difference of opinion was considered a boon and a healthy sign of life. The following saying is narrated in the preface to the *Durr Mukhtār* and in the *Fatāwā-i Tātār Khānīyyah.*

اختلاف ائمة الهدى توسعة للناس

["The difference of opinion amongst the *Imāms*, our leaders, provides latitude and wider scope to people."]

The Prophet himself has said: "If you find difference of opinion on any point among my Companions, you may follow any one of them." Caliph 'Umar b. 'Abd al-'Azīz has said : "These differences of opinion have provided us with great latitude in matters of religion. I consider this the most precious of all the valuable things in our faith. It would have been an extremely undesirable state of affairs if we were restricted to one and only one view in questions of this nature." The *Shāmī* says : "In case of necessity and with a view to making things easy for the Muslims, it would be advisable for a *Mufti* to give *Fatwā* according to the opinion of one jurist (belonging to any school) as against the opinions of other jurists." It is an almost unanimously accepted proposition that a judge belonging to one school of Muslim Law may decide a case according to the rules of any other school in case he finds that the view of his own school would create unnecessary hardship for both or one of the parties.

Taqlīd, A Later Development. As we have already seen, *Taqlīd* in its present form was not known or practised in the early history of Muslim Law. Abū Ṭālib Makkī, in his *Qūt al-Qulūb*, says : "To give *Fatwā* according to the system of jurisprudence founded by one man and to follow that system in all matters and in all respects was not in vogue in the first or the second century of the Hijri era." It was in the third century that Sunnī Muslims, who form an overwhelming majority of the Muslims of the world, began to adopt any one of the four schools of law (known as the *Madhāhib-i Arba'ah*) as their sole guide in all legal matters. During this period of our history some jurists continued doing *Ijtihād* on questions of details which came before them.

Door of Ijtihād Closed. But with the close of the third century Hijri era, the door of *Ijtihād* was finally closed. All the Sunnī Muslims of the world including jurists got divided into four sects, the Ḥanafīs, the Mālikīs, the Shāfi'īs and the Ḥanbalīs, and nothing was left for anybody but to follow and follow blindly. It was further ordained by good people like Ibn al-Ṣilāḥ, and others that it was not lawful for any person to follow any jurist other than one of the four *Imāms*, the founders of the four schools.

Shaikh 'Abd al-Wahhāb Sha'rānī says in the *Yawāqīt* : "So far our jurists have been following all the four *Imāms* indiscriminately without getting attached strictly to any one of the four schools." But gradually the jurists, and so the people in general, lined up in four different and distinct groups and began to follow their own school without caring much for the views of the other schools.

The result is that during the last ten centuries there has been no *Mujtahid Mustaqil* and consequently no *ijtihād*. Of course, two or three jurists did claim to be *Mujtahids* during this long period, but they were never accepted or recognised.

In the words of Ameer Ali :

"Unfortunately, the conception which has obtained a hold on the Sunnī world, that *ijtihād* or authoritative exposition of law by analogical deductions or the exercise of judgment ceased in the third century of the Hijri era, has exercised a most pernicious effect on the promotion and advancement of the Muhammadan communities governed by the Sunnī doctrines. . . . The *mujtahids* flourished in the first three centuries and the exercise of private judgment soon ceased to be acknowledged.

Some later doctors, Az-Zāhirī and Suyūṭī claimed the right, but public opinion rejected the claim. . . . The present stationary condition of the Muhammadan nations, as compared with their rapid progress in the early centuries of Islam, is due principally to this conception regarding *ijtihād.*"

Ghair Muqallid. Of course, there are some Sunnī Muslims who are against *Taqlīd.* They are a small minority and are called *Ghair Muqallids.* They say that :

"These blind followers do not know the man whom they are following. They do not know whether he is in the right or not, nor do they know where he is taking them. They know only so much that they are being led by someone. A *Muqallid* is like the person who was asked where he was going and he replied that he was going where the man ahead of him was going; and when asked again where the man ahead of him was going, he said he did not know."*

The Mu'tazilah. It has been said that as long as the Mu'tazilah (the Rationalists) had influence over the early 'Abbāsī rulers, *Taqlīd* did not gain any force. But with the downfall of this sect and coming to power of the followers of the Ḥanbalī school, blind *Taqlīd* gained prominence, and nothing was left for the scholars but to collect *aḥādīth,* relate them, explain the meanings of the words used in them and to state (following the scholars of old) whether a certain *Rāvī* was *thiqah* (sound) or *ḍa'īf* (weak), without any critical examination of the question. Likewise a jurist could not do anything more than to collect and follow the sayings of his *Imām,* and in case a new question of law cropped up, to

*Ibn Kathīr, *Tafsir.*

decide it in conformity with the general principles and rules framed by him.

In short, since the time of Mutawakkil, the 'Abbāsī Caliph, *Taqlīd* has always been the hard and fast rule of action, followed rigidly by everyone, not only in matters of law, but also in all other branches of learning. The result has been that most of the books, written and compiled during this period, on *Ḥadīth*, *Fiqh*, *Tafsīr*, *Ṣarf*, *Naḥw* and *Lughat*, etc., have followed older texts on these subjects.

The late Professor Browne, in his *A Literary History of Persia*, has very correctly depicted the position in this respect in the following words :

"Some learned man writes a theological, philological or logical treatise which achieves renown in the college where the '*Ulama* get their mediaeval training. Someone else writes a commentary on that treatise; a third produces a super-commentary on the commentary; a fourth, a gloss on the super-commentary; a fifth, a note on the gloss; so that at the end we are confronted with what the immortal Turkish wit Khwaja Nasruddin Efendi called 'soup of the soup of the soup of the hare-soup, a substance devoid of savour or nutriment, and serving rather to conceal than to reveal its original material. Shaikh Muhammad Abduhu, late Grand Mufti of Egypt and Chancellor of the University of Al-Azhar, . . . used to say that all this stuff should be burned, since it merely cumbered book-shelves, bread maggots, and obscured sound knowledge."

Part Two

THE QURANIC LAW OF CRIMES

"And it becometh not s believing man or a believing woman, when Allah and His messenger have decided an affair (for them) that they should (after that) claim any say in their affair. And whoso disobeys Allah and His messenger, he verily goeth astray in error manifest" (Qur. xxxiii. 36).

INTRODUCTION

Under Muslim Law, criminal cases are of two kinds: (1) *Ḥadd* cases, which relate to offences for which punishment is prescribed by law. There are only a few offences which fall under this head. (2) *Ta'zīr* cases, which relate to offences for which no punishment is prescribed by law. In these cases, the judge is left free to sentence the accused to any punishment he deems fit under the circumstances of each case. All cases of crimes, excepting six or seven *Ḥadd* cases, come under this head.

The above definitions are based on the definitions of these words given in the *Ḥidāyah*, the most popular and standard text-book of Muslim Law.

It this part, we will deal with the *Ḥadd* offences mentioned in the Qur'ān.

Chapter 1

ADULTERY

Definition of Adultery under Muslim Law. A man who has sexual intercourse with a woman who is not his wife and a woman who has such intercourse with a man who is not her husband are guilty of adultery and are both liable to punishment.

Definition of Adultery under P.P.C. The offence of adultery is defined in the Pakistan Penal Code in Section 497, which says :

> "Whoever has sexual intercourse with a person who is and whom he knows or has reason to believe to be the wife of another man, without the consent or connivance of that man . . . is guilty of the offence of adultery. . . ."

Difference between the Two Definitions. From a careful perusal of the two definitions, we see that under the Pakistan Penal Code, sexual intercourse with an unmarried woman or a widow or a divorced woman and such intercourse with the wife of another person with his consent or connivance is no offence. We also see that the woman concerned in the act of adultery is guilty of no offence.

On the other hand, under Muslim Law, sexual intercourse in all the above cases is an offence and both the man and the woman are liable to punishment.

Proof of Adultery. Ordinarily, under Muslim Law,

two witnesses are required to prove a fact. In some cases only one witness can prove it. But in case of adultery, no less than four witnesses are required to prove the offence. The Quranic verses cited below are authority for this proposition of the Muslim Law of evidence. Muslim jurists go further and say that all the four witnesses must be eye-witnesses of actual penetration.

Confession. The admission of adultery by the accused can also prove the offence. According to the Ḥanafī school of Muslim jurisprudence, such admission must be made at four different times and in four different sittings. The judge has to turn the accused out and away from his presence after the first, second and third admission. The Ḥanafīs base their opinion on the case of one Mā'iz heard and decided by the Prophet himself, and also on the analogy of four witnesses. But Shāfi'ī says that admission made by the accused once is sufficient to prove the case against him.

Less than Four Witnesses. It is worth notice here that less than four witnesses not only do not prove the offence of adultery, but are also considered to be false witnesses even if they be telling the truth. The *Hidāyah* says :

> "If less than four witnesses give evidence of adultery against somebody, their evidence shall be rejected and they shall be punished for bringing a false charge of adultery."

A person who accuses a woman of adultery and cannot prove the fact by evidence of four witnesses shall be deemed to be a liar in the eye of law (even if the accusation be true in fact). The Qur'ān says :

لَوْلَا جَاءُوْ عَلَيْهِ بِأَرْبَعَةِ شُهَدَآءَ فَإِذْ لَمْ يَأْتُوا
بِالشُّهَدَآءِ فَأُولٰٓئِكَ عِنْدَ اللّٰهِ هُمُ الْكٰذِبُوْنَ

["Why did they not bring four witnesses of it? So, as they have not brought witnesses they are liars in the sight of Allah" (xxiv. 13).]

As a matter of fact, the Qur'ān very strongly deprecates the publication of sexual scandal and calumny among the Muslims. It says :

إِنَّ الَّذِيْنَ يُحِبُّوْنَ أَنْ تَشِيْعَ
الْفَاحِشَةُ فِي الَّذِيْنَ اٰمَنُوْا لَهُمْ عَذَابٌ أَلِيْمٌ فِي الدُّنْيَا وَالْاٰخِرَةِ

["Those who love that (sexual) scandal should circulate respecting Muslims, for them is a grievous chastisement in this world and the world hereafter" (xxiv. 19).]

It is therefore that special provisions have been made in the law of evidence regardiug adultery cases.

Punishment. The following is the first Quranic verse revealed in this connection :

وَالّٰتِيْ يَأْتِيْنَ الْفَاحِشَةَ مِنْ نِّسَآئِكُمْ فَاسْتَشْهِدُوْا عَلَيْهِنَّ
أَرْبَعَةً مِّنْكُمْ فَإِنْ شَهِدُوْا فَأَمْسِكُوْهُنَّ فِي الْبُيُوْتِ حَتّٰى
يَتَوَفّٰهُنَّ الْمَوْتُ أَوْ يَجْعَلَ اللّٰهُ لَهُنَّ سَبِيْلًا

["And as for those of your women who are guilty of adultery, call to witness against them four (witnesses) from among you, so if they bear witness, confine them to the houses until death takes them away or Allah makes a way for them" (iv. 15),]

Thus we see that house confinement for life was the punishment for adultery, given to a woman under this verse. But the verse itself says that some other provision may be made in this respect in future. This other provision was in fact made in the following Quranic verse :

اَلزَّانِيَةُ وَالزَّانِيْ فَاجْلِدُوْا كُلَّ وَاحِدٍ مِّنْهُمَا مِائَةَ
جَلْدَةٍ وَّلَا تَاْخُذْكُمْ بِهِمَا رَاْفَةٌ فِيْ دِيْنِ اللّٰهِ اِنْ كُنْتُمْ
تُؤْمِنُوْنَ بِاللّٰهِ وَالْيَوْمِ الْاٰخِرِ وَلْيَشْهَدْ عَذَابَهُمَا طَآئِفَةٌ مِّنَ
الْمُؤْمِنِيْنَ

["The adulteress and the adulterer, flog each of them (with) a hundred stripes, and let not pity for them detain you from obedience to Allah, if you believe in Allah and the Last day, and let a party of Muslims witness their chastisement" (xxiv. 2).]

The only other verse in the Qur'ān relating to the question of punishment for adultery is the one which says :

" Then if they (the slave-girls) are guilty of adultery when they are taken in marriage, they shall suffer half the punishment (prescribed) for free women" (iv. 25).

Now it is abundantly clear from what has been said, that according to the Qur'ān, the punishment for adultery for both man and woman is a hundred stripes inflicted in public in the presence of a party of Muslims.

Rajm. But almost all Muslim jurists say that this punishment is for unmarried people. According to the *Hidāyah* : "When a married person is convicted of adultery, he (or she) shall be sentenced to *Rajm*, i.e. to be stoned to death. The authority for this is the case of Mā'iz. This case is mentioned, in detail, in the following *ḥadīth* :

"Buraidah says: Mā'iz son of Mālik came to the Prophet and said: 'Make me clean.' The Prophet said: 'Woe to thee, go back, ask for God's pardon and repent before Him.' The man went away a short distance and returned and again said: 'Make me clean.' The Prophet gave him the same reply as he had given in the first instance. The man went away, came back again, said the same thing, got the same reply and went away. He returned for the fourth time and said: 'Make me clean.' The Prophet said: 'Of what should I make you clean?' The man replied: 'Of adultery.' The Prophet said: 'Is the man mad?' People said he was not. The Prophet then asked: 'Has the man taken some intoxicant?' Thereupon a man stood up, smelled the mouth of Mā'iz and said: 'No! he is not drunk.' The Prophet asked the man: 'Have you committed adultery?' He replied: 'Yes!' The Prophet then ordered that the man should be stoned to death and so he was. . . ." (*Mishkat*, Bk. XVI, Ch. 1).

There is nothing on record to show that the case of Mā'iz occurred after the above-cited verses of the Qur'ān concerning the punishment for adultery were revealed. It is stated that a *Ṣaḥābī* (Companion of the Prophet) was once asked whether the case of Mā'iz was before or after the verse prescribing a hundred stripes as punishment for adultery was revealed. He replied: "I do not know." It is submitted that if this tradition is genuine, the case of Mā'iz must have been decided before the Quranic verse was revealed.

Moreover, it has been stated in the *Uṣūl al-Shāshī*, a well-known book on Muslim jurisprudence, that the Mā'iz tradition was, in the early period of Islamic history, of the nature of a *Khabar-i Wāḥid* which is the weakest kind of a *ḥadīth*. It was in the later period that the tradition became *Mashhūr*.

It may be noted here that many of our jurists hold that the Quranic verse (xxiv. 2) stands repealed by the above *ḥadīth*. To say that the word of God can be abrogated by the word of the Prophet is, to say the least, saying too much. Man-worship always creeps in through such crevices.

Biblical Law. It is in evidence that the Prophet decided several cases according to the Law of Moses when there was no Quranic ordinance on the point involved in the case.

Now, according to the Biblical Law, stoning to death is the punishment for adultery, as the following verses from the Bible would show :

"13. If any man take a wife, and go in unto her, and hate her. . . .

"14. . . . and say . . . I found her not a maid : . . .

"20. But if this thing be true, and the tokens of virginity be not found for the damsel:

"21. Then they shall bring out the damsel to the door of her father's house, and the men of her city shall stone her with stones that she die. . . .

"22. If a man be found lying with a woman married to a husband, then they shall both of them die. . . .

"23. If a damsel that is a virgin be betrothed unto a husband, and a man find her in the city, and lie with her;

"24. Then ye shall bring them both out unto the gate of that city, and ye shall stone them with stones that they die; . . ." (Deuteronomy, 22 : 13-24).

It may be noted here that a minority of Muslim jurists have always held the opinion that the only punishment for adultery of all kinds is a hundred stripes and that *Rajm* is based on no authority. Most of the modern Muslim jurists and scholars have expressed the same opinion.

It is also worth notice that the majority of our

jurists, who are in favour of *Rajm*, have on the other hand so enunciated the law of evidence on the point that it has become almost impossible to sentence a person to *Rajm* unless he or she, like Mā'īz, insists on being stoned to death.

Forgiveness. Shāfi'ī says that the exception, in favour of those offenders who repent and reform themselves, made by the Qur'ān in connection with certain offences, may apply to all offences. In one of the versions of Mā'iz's story, it is said that when people began to throw stones at him, he ran away. He was overtaken and stoned to death. When the Prophet was informed of all this, he said : "Why did you not let him go? " (*Mishkāt*, Bk. XVI. Ch. 1).

Chapter 2

FALSE CHARGE OF ADULTERY

The following Quranic verses relate to the offence of false charge of adultery against a person :

وَالَّذِينَ يَرْمُونَ الْمُحْصَنٰتِ ثُمَّ لَمْ يَأْتُوا بِأَرْبَعَةِ شُهَدَاءَ
فَاجْلِدُوهُمْ ثَمٰنِينَ جَلْدَةً وَلَا تَقْبَلُوا لَهُمْ شَهَادَةً أَبَدًا ۚ
وَأُولٰٓئِكَ هُمُ الْفٰسِقُونَ ﴿٤﴾ إِلَّا الَّذِينَ تَابُوا مِنْ بَعْدِ ذٰلِكَ وَ
أَصْلَحُوا ۚ فَإِنَّ اللّٰهَ غَفُورٌ رَّحِيمٌ

["And those who accuse chaste women but bring not four witnesses, scourge them (with) eighty stripes and never (afterwards) accept their testimony. They indeed are evil-doers: save those who afterward repent and reform themselves. Surely Allah is Forgiving, Merciful" (xxiv. 4-5).]

The plain meaning of these verses is that a charge of adultery against a chaste woman, even if true, shall be deemed false unless it is supported by four witnesses.

False Charge Against A Man. The above verses relate to a false charge of adultery against a woman, but the majority of our jurists say that by way of *Qiyās* the verses apply to a false charge of that nature against a man as well.

Punishment. The punishment for this offence is twofold : (1) The offender shall be flogged (with) eighty stripes and (2) his evidence shall not be accepted in any case, in future.

Difference of Opinion. Shāfi'ī says that after the offender has repented and reformed himself, his evidence may be accepted in future cases. Rāzī says that the majority of the Companions of the Prophet and the Successors held the same opinion. But according to Ḥanafī jurists, his evidence cannot be accepted even after his repentance.

Charge Against A Non-Muslim. It has been said that the word *muḥṣanah* used in the verse means a chaste Muslim woman. Therefore a false charge of adultery against a non-Muslim man or woman is not punishable by way of *Ḥadd.* It can be punished by way of *Ta'zīr.*

Unchaste Woman. It has been said that a false charge of adultery against a man or woman who is not chaste is also punishable by way of *Tā'zīr* only. But a false charge against a person who is notorious for adultery is not punishable at all.

Ta'zīr Punishment. The *Hidāyah* says:

> "The maximum number of stripes in *ta'zīr* punishment is thirty-nine and the minimum three. But the judge may add a sentence of imprisonment as well.
>
> "Some jurists say that the maximum is seventy-nine stripes."

Deemed False. The following Quranic verse is a direct authority for the proposition that a charge of adultery unsupported by four witnesses shall be deemed false:

لَوْلَا جَاءُوْ عَلَيْهِ بِأَرْبَعَةِ شُهَدَاءَ ۚ فَإِذْ لَمْ يَأْتُوا
بِالشُّهَدَاءِ فَأُولَٰئِكَ عِنْدَ اللَّهِ هُمُ الْكَاذِبُونَ

["Why did they not bring four witnesses of it? So, as they

have not brought witnesses, they are liars in the sight of Allah" (xiv. 13).]

Li'ān Proceedings. It may be noted here that the Qur'ān makes an exception in favour of the husband who brings a charge of adultery against his wife. They shall take *Li'ān* proceedings. If the husband recites the *Li'ān* formula, he will escape punishment for false charge of adultery ; and if the wife recites her part of the formula, she will be saved from punishment for adultery. The Qur'ān says :

وَالَّذِيْنَ يَرْمُوْنَ اَزْوَاجَهُمْ
وَلَمْ يَكُنْ لَّهُمْ شُهَدَآءُ اِلَّآ اَنْفُسُهُمْ فَشَهَادَةُ اَحَدِهِمْ اَرْبَعُ
شَهٰدٰتٍ بِاللّٰهِ اِنَّهٗ لَمِنَ الصّٰدِقِيْنَ ۝ وَالْخَامِسَةُ اَنَّ لَعْنَتَ
اللّٰهِ عَلَيْهِ اِنْ كَانَ مِنَ الْكٰذِبِيْنَ ۝ وَيَدْرَؤُا عَنْهَا الْعَذَابَ
اَنْ تَشْهَدَ اَرْبَعَ شَهٰدٰتٍ بِاللّٰهِ اِنَّهٗ لَمِنَ الْكٰذِبِيْنَ ۝
وَالْخَامِسَةَ اَنَّ غَضَبَ اللّٰهِ عَلَيْهَآ اِنْ كَانَ مِنَ الصّٰدِقِيْنَ ۝

["And those who accuse their wives and have no witnesses except themselves, let one of them testify four times, bearing Allah to witness, that he is of those who speak the truth, and the fifth time that the curse of Allah be on him if he is of those who lie. And it shall avert punishment from her, if she testify four times, bearing Allah to witness, that he is of those who lie. And the fifth time, that the wrath of Allah be on her, if he is of those who speak the truth" (xxiv. 6-9).]

After these proceedings, the judge shall order separation between the parties, which practically means divorce.

Chapter 3

SODOMY AND OTHER UNNATURAL OFFENCES

Definition. Pakistan Penal Code defines unnatural offences in these words: "Carnal intercourse against the order of nature with any man, woman or animal" (Sec. 377). The offence consists in sexual intercourse committed against the order of nature by a man with a man, or in the same unnatural manner with a woman, or by a man or a woman with a beast in any manner. The same is the definition of the offence under Muslim Law.

The following is the Quranic verse relating to this offence :

وَالَّذٰنِ يَأْتِيٰنِهَا

مِنْكُمْ فَاٰذُوْهُمَا ۚ فَاِنْ تَابَا وَاَصْلَحَا فَاَعْرِضُوْا عَنْهُمَا ۗ اِنَّ اللّٰهَ

كَانَ تَوَّابًا رَّحِيْمًا

["And as for those two men of you who are guilty thereof (i.e. of unlawful intercourse mentioned in the last preceding verse), punish them both. And if they repent and improve, then turn aside from them. Surely Allah is Relenting, Merciful" (iv. 16).]

Difference of Opinion. Some of our jurists and commentators hold the opinion that like the preceding verse (Q. iv. 15), this verse, as well, relates to the offence of adultery. They say that the word *Walla-*

dhān which literally means "those two men," may also, under the rules of Arabic grammar, mean a man and a woman. Another instance of this is the word *Wālidain* which literally means "two fathers" but actually means the father and the mother, the parents.

On the other hand, some of our jurists say that the verse relates to unnatural offences.

Punishment. The Qur'ān has left the question of punishment open and the judge may, in the exercise of his discretion, pass any sentence he deems proper. The *Hidāyah* says :

> "In the case of a person who commits sodomy, no *Ḥadd* punishment is fixed. The offender shall be punished by way of *Ta'zīr*. It is so according to Abū Ḥanīfah. It has been said in *Jāmi' al-Ṣaghīr* that the offender shall be detained in prison till he repents and reforms himself. Abū Yūsuf and Muḥammad say that the act is punishable as adultery. Shāfi'ī agrees with Abū Yūsuf and Muḥammad.
>
> "*Ḥadd* punishment for carnal intercourse with an animal has not been fixed. The offender shall be punished by way of *Ta'zīr*."

Two Objectionable Words. The words *Liwāṭat* meaning sodomy and *Lūṭī* meaning a sodomite are the most objectionable words ever coined. To bring in the name of a Prophet of God (vi. 2), Lot, in the formation of these words is nothing but blasphemy.

Alternatives Suggested. The words "sodomy," which means the act of an inhabitant of Sodom, and "sodomite" are the proper words to be used in this connection. Therefore it is submitted that for the word *Liwāṭat* we should use the word *Sudumiyat* and for the word *Lūṭī* we should use the word *Sidūmī* in future.

The only other *Ḥadd* punishment case under Muslim Law is the one relating to the offence of going out drunk. But there is nothing about it in the Qur'ān. The Prophet used to flog people for this offence but fixed no number of stripes. The number (forty and later eighty) was fixed by the Companions after him.

All other offences are *Ta'zir* cases and the question of punishment is left open for the legislature of the country or the judges to decide.

Chapter 4

MURDER, CULPABLE HOMICIDE NOT AMOUNTING TO MURDER, AND HURT

According to Muslim Law, there are three main kinds of culpable homicide: (*a*) *Qatl-i ʻAmd*, i.e. wilful murder; (*b*) *Qatl-i ʻShibh-i ʻAmd*, i.e. homicide resembling wilful murder, and (*c*) *Qatl-i Khaṭā'*, i.e. homicide by mistake.

(1) *Qatl-i ʻAmd* is defined in the *Ḥidāyah* in the following words:

"If a person intentionally strikes another person with a weapon (e.g. a sword, or a spear, etc.) or with something which amounts to a weapon, e.g. a sharp wood, a sharp stone or fire, and kills him, he is said to have committed wilful murder."

(2) *Qatl-i Shibh-i ʻAmd* is defined in the same book in these terms:

"According to Abū Ḥanīfah: If a person intentionally strikes another person with something which is not a weapon nor amounts to a weapon (e.g., a stick or a stone, etc.) and kills him, he is said to have committed homicide resembling wilful murder. But according to Abū Yūsuf, Muḥammad and Shāfiʻī: if the person uses a big stone or a big piece of wood (e.g. a big stick) he commits wilful murder. According to them, a person commits homicide resembling wilful murder only when he uses something which does not ordinarily cause death."

We see from these definitions that the determining factor, in the question whether the offence is "culpable homicide amounting to murder" or "culpable homicide not amounting to murder," is the nature of the weapon used. If death is caused with a firearm, a sharp-edged or a sharp-pointed weapon or fire, it is wilful murder; if it is caused with a blunt weapon, such as a stick or stone, it is culpable homicide not amounting to murder.

It may be noted here that what Muslim Law calls "wilful murder" is called "murder" in the Pakistan Penal Code; and "homicide resembling wilful murder" is called "culpable homicide not amounting to murder".

(3) *Qatl-i Khaṭā'* is described by the *Hidāyah* as follows:

> "Mistake is of two kinds: (*i*) mistake of intention, e.g. a man darts an arrow on something which he thinks is an animal, but which in fact is a human being and kills him, or throws a missile on a person whom he thinks one of those at war with the Muslims but who in fact is a Muslim and kills him, and (*ii*) mistake of act, e.g. a person darts a missile at the target but it hits a man, who is killed.
>
> "In these cases the man is guilty of 'homicide by mistake'. But a person who intentionally aims a blow at one part of the deceased's body but hits another part and kills him is guilty of wilful murder."

Punishment for Qatl-i 'Amd is given in the Qur'ān in the following verses:

يٰٓاَيُّهَا الَّذِيْنَ
اٰمَنُوْا كُتِبَ عَلَيْكُمُ الْقِصَاصُ فِى الْقَتْلٰى ؕ اَلْحُرُّ بِالْحُرِّ وَالْعَبْدُ
بِالْعَبْدِ وَالْاُنْثٰى بِالْاُنْثٰى ؕ فَمَنْ عُفِىَ لَهٗ مِنْ اَخِيْهِ شَىْءٌ
فَاتِّبَاعٌ ۢ بِالْمَعْرُوْفِ وَاَدَآءٌ اِلَيْهِ بِاِحْسَانٍ ؕ ذٰلِكَ تَخْفِيْفٌ
مِّنْ رَّبِّكُمْ وَرَحْمَةٌ ؕ فَمَنِ اعْتَدٰى بَعْدَ ذٰلِكَ فَلَهٗ عَذَابٌ
اَلِيْمٌ ۝ وَلَكُمْ فِى الْقِصَاصِ حَيٰوةٌ يّٰٓاُولِى الْاَلْبَابِ لَعَلَّكُمْ
تَتَّقُوْنَ

["O ye who believe! retaliation is prescribed for you in the matter of the murdered. . . . And for him who is forgiven somewhat by his (aggrieved) brother, prosecution (for blood-money) should be according to usage and payment unto him in kindness. This is an alleviation and a mercy from your Lord. He who transgresseth after this will have a painful chastisement. And there is life for you in relaliation, O men of understanding, that you may ward off (evil)" (ii. 178-79).]

Qiṣāṣ means retaliation, i.e. if the accused has committed *Qatl-i 'Amd*, he is liable to be sentenced to death and if he has caused hurt to someone, he is liable to receive a like hurt.

According to the above Quranic verses, the heirs of the deceased may :

(*a*) demand that the murderer be sentenced to death, or

(*b*) demand that he be made to pay *Diyat*, i.e. blood-money, or

(*c*) forgive him altogether.

The following *ḥadīth* also bears upon the point :

" . . . The Prophet said: He who commits wilful murder shall be handed over to the heirs of the deceased, and they may kill him if they like or may accept blood-money if they so choose . . ." (*Mishkāt*, Bk. XV. Ch. 1).

Diyat or *Khūn Bahā* means blood-money. In the time of the Prophet *Diyat* was fixed at one hundred camels or their market price, 8000 dirhams. Later 'Umar raised it to 12,000 dirhams, because, he said, the price of camel had gone up.

Dirham was a silver coin weighing a little more than our old four-anna silver piece. Thus 12,000 dirhams would mean about 3300 tolas of silver.

But the amount of *Diyat* today would be the present market-value of one hundred camels.

It is worth notice here that, under Muslim Law, all the agnatic relations of the murderer are liable to pay the *Diyat*.

Diyat Paid from the Bait al-Māl. A *ḥadīth* narrated both by Bukhārī and Muslim says :

" 'Abd Allah son of Sahl was killed while at Khaibar by some Jew. The occurrence was not witnessed by anybody. The relation of the deceased came to the Prophet and informed him of the murder. As the offender was not known, the Prophet gave one hundred camels to the heirs of the deceased, by way of *Diyat* (from the Bait al-Māl)" (*Mishkāt*, Bk. XV, Ch. 4).

Punishment for *Qatl-i Shibh-i 'Amd*, i.e. culpable homicide not amounting to murder, is the same as for *Qatl-i Khaṭā'* (*Hidāyah*).

Punishment for Qatl-i Khaṭā' is given in the following Quranic verse :

وَمَنْ قَتَلَ مُؤْمِنًا خَطَأً فَتَحْرِيرُ رَقَبَةٍ مُّؤْمِنَةٍ وَّدِيَةٌ
مُّسَلَّمَةٌ إِلَىٰٓ أَهْلِهِۦٓ إِلَّآ أَنْ يَصَّدَّقُوا۟ ۚ فَإِنْ كَانَ مِنْ قَوْمٍ عَدُوٍّ
لَّكُمْ وَهُوَ مُؤْمِنٌ فَتَحْرِيرُ رَقَبَةٍ مُّؤْمِنَةٍ ۖ وَإِنْ كَانَ مِنْ قَوْمٍۭ
بَيْنَكُمْ وَبَيْنَهُمْ مِّيثَٰقٌ فَدِيَةٌ مُّسَلَّمَةٌ إِلَىٰٓ أَهْلِهِۦ وَتَحْرِيرُ
رَقَبَةٍ مُّؤْمِنَةٍ ۖ فَمَنْ لَّمْ يَجِدْ فَصِيَامُ شَهْرَيْنِ مُتَتَابِعَيْنِ
تَوْبَةً مِّنَ ٱللَّهِ ۗ وَكَانَ ٱللَّهُ عَلِيمًا حَكِيمًا ﴿٩٢﴾

["And he who kills a Musiim by mistake should free a Muslim slave, and blood-money should be paid to his people unless they remit it as alms. But if he be from a tribe hostile to you and he is a Muslim, the freeing of a Muslim slave (suffices). And if he be from a tribe between whom and you there is a covenant, the blood-money should be paid to his people along with the freeing of a Muslim slave; but he who has not the means should fast for two months successively: a penance from Allah. And Allah is Ever-Knowing, Wise" (iv. 92).]

We see that the punishment prescribed here includes both the punishment for the crime and the *Kaffārah* for the sin. The freeing of a slave is by way of *Kaffārah*, "but he who has not the means should fast two months".

We also see that *Diyat* is not payable when the person killed belongs to a hostile tribe. The reason seems to be that money from a Muslim State should not go to an enemy country.

Punishment for Hurt is given in the following Quranic verse :

وَكَتَبْنَا عَلَيْهِمْ فِيهَا أَنَّ النَّفْسَ بِالنَّفْسِ وَ
الْعَيْنَ بِالْعَيْنِ وَالْأَنْفَ بِالْأَنْفِ وَالْأُذُنَ بِالْأُذُنِ وَ
السِّنَّ بِالسِّنِّ وَالْجُرُوحَ قِصَاصٌ فَمَنْ تَصَدَّقَ بِهِ فَهُوَ
كَفَّارَةٌ لَهُ وَمَنْ لَمْ يَحْكُمْ بِمَا أَنْزَلَ اللَّهُ
فَأُولَٰئِكَ هُمُ الظَّالِمُونَ

["And We prescribed for them (i.e. the Jews) therein (i.e. in the Torah) that: Life is for life, and eye for eye, and nose for nose, and ear for ear, and tooth for tooth. and for wounds retaliation. But whoso forgoes it (in the way of charity), it shall be expiation for him. And whoever judges not by what Allah has revealed, those are unjust" (v. 45).]

The above Quranic verse refers to the following Biblical verses :

"And if any mischief follow, then thou shalt give life for life, Eye for eye, tooth for tooth, hand for hand, foot for foot, Burning for burning, wound for wound; stripe for stripe" (Exodus, 21 :]23-25).

It is a well-known principle of Muslim jurisprudence that when an old God-given law is mentioned in the Qur'ān or the *Ḥadīth*, and is not expressly amended or repealed, it is good law for us. Thus the above Biblical law, prescribing punishment for hurt, is the law we follow.

According to this law, *Qiṣāṣ* is ordained for all cases of hurt. If a person knocks out the tooth of another person, his tooth shall be knocked out. If a person gives a blow at the eye of another person and the eyesight is gone, the offender shall be deprived of his eyesight in *Qiṣāṣ*. In all cases of injury, wounds, etc., the offender shall be liable to receive exactly the same injury.

But in cases in which it is not possible to inflict exactly the same injury upon the offender, and in cases where such an injury involves the risk of serious consequences such as death, etc., *Qiṣāṣ* is not allowed. In these cases, *Diyat* shall be awarded to the complainant, the amount of which may be determined by the judge. Our jurists have fixed the amount in many cases.

Injury Forgiven Before Death. If the person who is injured forgives the offender and later dies of the same injury, the offender shall be liable to pay the *Diyat*. But if the injured person forgave the offender both for the injury and for its consequences, no *Diyat* shall be payable (*Hidāyah*).

Injury Punished Before Death. If a person injures another person and is punished in *Qiṣāṣ* (either by receiving a like injury or by paying the *Diyat*) and the injured person later dies of the same injury, the offender shall be liable to *Qiṣāṣ* for murder (*Hidāyah*).

Injury Given in Qiṣāṣ Causes Death. If a person causes an injury to another person in *Qiṣāṣ* (of his own injury) and the person so injured dies of the injury, the person causing the injury in *Qiṣāṣ* shall be liable to pay *Dîyat*. It is so according to Abū Ḥanīfah, but Abū Yūsuf and Muḥammad say that no *Diyat* is payable in this case (*Hidāyah*).

It may be noted that under Muslim Law, the offender is handed over to the heirs of the deceased or to the complainant for the execution of *Qiṣāṣ*, in cases of murder or hurt.

Chapter 5

REBELLION, WAGING WAR AGAINST THE STATE AND HIGHWAY ROBBERY OR DACOITY WITH OR WITHOUT MURDER

The law relating to rebellion and highway robbery, etc., is given in the following verses of the Qur'ān :

إِنَّمَا جَزَٰٓؤُا ٱلَّذِينَ يُحَارِبُونَ
ٱللَّهَ وَرَسُولَهُۥ وَيَسْعَوْنَ فِى ٱلْأَرْضِ
فَسَادًا أَن يُقَتَّلُوٓا أَوْ يُصَلَّبُوٓا أَوْ تُقَطَّعَ أَيْدِيهِمْ وَأَرْجُلُهُم
مِّنْ خِلَٰفٍ أَوْ يُنفَوْا مِنَ ٱلْأَرْضِ ذَٰلِكَ لَهُمْ خِزْىٌ فِى ٱلدُّنْيَا
وَلَهُمْ فِى ٱلْءَاخِرَةِ عَذَابٌ عَظِيمٌ ﴿٣٣﴾ إِلَّا ٱلَّذِينَ تَابُوا مِن قَبْلِ
أَن تَقْدِرُوا عَلَيْهِمْ فَٱعْلَمُوٓا أَنَّ ٱللَّهَ غَفُورٌ رَّحِيمٌ ﴿٣٤﴾ يَٰٓأَيُّهَا ٱلَّذِينَ

["The only reward of those who make war upon Allah and His Messenger and strive to create mischief and horror in the land will be that they will be killed or crucified, or have their hands and feet on alternate sides cut off, or will be expelled out of the land (or imprisoned). Such will be their degradation in the world, and in the Hereafter theirs will be an awful doom; save those who repent before you overpower them. For know that Allah is Forgiving, Merciful" (v. 33-34).]

The word *fasād* used in these verses means mischief, horror, grave or widespread breach of public peace, mutiny, sedition, riotous tumult, etc.

The word *yunfau* is made from the root-word (*nafī*) which means both "banishing or exiling and imprisoning.

The Qur'ān ordains the following punishments for the offences of this nature : (*a*) to slay, or (*b*) to crucify, or (*c*) to cut off one hand and one foot on the opposite sides, i.e. the right hand and the left foot or the left hand and the right foot, or (*d*) to banish, or (*e*) to imprison.

Therefore it is open to the judge to pass any one of these sentences which he thinks fit under the circumstances of each case.

Our jurists have suggested the following punishments under the following circumstances :

(1) Murder committed and property robbed : Crucifixion.

(2) Murder committed but no property robbed : Death sentence.

(3) No murder committed but property robbed : Cutting off a hand and a foot.

(4) No murder committed, no property robbed : Exile or imprisonment.

This apportionment of punishment may be considered just as a guide. No hard and fast rules could be made in this conneetion, because the circumstances of each case and the liability of each accused differ very widely in different cases.

Crucifixion. There is a difference of opinion about the method of crucifixion. Most of the Ḥanafī jurists say that the convict shall be fastened to the crucifix alive and then killed there with a spear, and the body to remain there for more than three days. Ṭaḥāwī says that he shall first be killed and then put on the gibbet. Shāfi'ī also holds the same opinion.

Constructive Liability. The *Hidāyah* says :

"If one of the party commits murder, all of them shall be liable to the same punishment as he. This is so because all of them had gone out with a common object."

This corresponds to Section 149 of the Pakistan Penal Code which says :

"If an offence is committed by any member of an unlawful assembly in prosecution of the common object of that assembly, or such as the members of that assembly know to be likely to be committed in prosecution of that object, every person who, at the time of the committing of that offence, is a member of the same assembly, is guilty of that offence."

Section 396 of the Pakistan Penal Code is more directly in point. It reads as follows :

"If any one of five or more persons, who are conjointly committing dacoity, commits murder in so committing dacoity, every one of those persons shall be punished with death or. . . ."

Section 34 of the Pakistan Penal Code may also be seen in this connection.

Highway Robbery. According to the majority of Muslim jurists, the above Quranic verses apply only to highway robbery and not to all robberies. The *Hidāyah* says :

"Robbery by day or night, in or near a town, is not highway robbery. This is by way of *Istiḥsān*, though by way of *Qiyās* it is to be treated as a highway robbery and Shāfi'ī treats it as such. Abū Yūsuf says that a robbery outside a town though near it is highway robbery.

"The offenders in case of a robbery in or near a town, though not liable to *Ḥadd* punishment, may be imprisoned by way of *Ta'zīr*. They shall also be liable to return the stolen property or to pay compensation for it and if one of them has committed a murder, he may be killed by the heirs of the deceased, unless they forgive him.

"It is stated in the *Fatḥ al-Qadīr* that the Ḥanafī judges follow Abū Yūsuf in this matter."

Application of the Verses. Some of our jurists say that these Quranic verses apply only to non-Muslims. But most of them are of opinion that the verses do apply to Muslims as well.

Repentance. The last sentence of these verses creates an exception in favour of the culprit who is not arrested soon after the occurrence but long after it. It is said that if in the meanwhile he has repented and reformed himself, he may be forgiven.

This shows that punishment for crimes under Muslim Law is with the purpose of reforming the offender and not in vindictiveness. Emperor Aurangzeb in his *Farmān* to his judges says, in case of many offences, that the offender should be sentenced to remain in prison till the time he reforms himself.

Fakhr al-Dīn Rāzī in his *Tafsīr-i Kabīr* says that, according to Shāfi'ī, this exception may apply to all criminal cases.

Rights of Man. But our jurists say that the forgiveness relates only to *Ḥuqūq Allah*, i.e. the rights of God, and does not relate to *Ḥuqūq al-'Ibād*, i.e. the rights of men. The *Hidāyah* says :

"If an offender, who had murdered someone at the time of occurrence, is arrested after he has repented and reformed himself, he shall not be liable to *Ḥadd* punishment, but the heirs of the deceased shall have the right to kill him or to forgive him."

It is noteworthy that the punishment of crucifixion and cutting of one hand and one foot on opposite sides was in vogue as far back as the time of Moses'

Pharaoh, as would appear from the following Quranic verse :

فَلَأُقَطِّعَنَّ أَيْدِيَكُمْ وَأَرْجُلَكُم مِّنْ خِلَافٍ وَلَأُصَلِّبَنَّكُمْ فِي
جُذُوعِ النَّخْلِ

["(Addressing the enchanters Pharaoh said :) Therefore I will cut off your hands and your feet on opposite sides, and I will crucify you on the trunks of the palm trees" (xx. 71).]

Chapter 6

THEFT

The Quranic law prescribing punishment for theft is given in the following verses :

وَالسَّارِقُ
وَالسَّارِقَةُ فَاقْطَعُوٓا أَيْدِيَهُمَا جَزَآءًۢ بِمَا كَسَبَا نَكَالًا مِّنَ
اللّٰهِ ۗ وَاللّٰهُ عَزِيزٌ حَكِيمٌ ۝ فَمَنْ تَابَ مِنۢ بَعْدِ ظُلْمِهٖ وَأَصْلَحَ
فَإِنَّ اللّٰهَ يَتُوبُ عَلَيْهِ ۗ إِنَّ اللّٰهَ غَفُورٌ رَّحِيمٌ

[“If a man or a woman steal, cut off their hands, in retribution for that which they have committed. This is an exemplary punishment appointed by God; and God is Mighty and Wise. But whoever shall repent after his iniquity, and reform himself, verily God will turn to him, for God is inclined to forgive, and Merciful” (v. 38-39).]

Punishment. We see that the punishment for theft ordained by the Qur'ān is that the hand of the thief shall be cut off. Our jurists say that this is the only punishment which can be awarded in a theft case. No other punishment, according to them, is possible in any case of theft.

Amputation, the Maximum Punishment. It is submitted that this view of our jurists is based on a grave misunderstanding. Like all other Penal Codes of the world, the Qur'ān mentions the maximum punishment for an offence and it is not at all necessary for a judge to award that punishment in each and every case. The facts and the attending circumstances of each case are different and in some cases they are so far different from each other as the two poles are. It does not stand to reason, therefore, that in all cases for a particular offence, the punishment should be one and the same.

That this is so is borne out by the Qur'ān, the *Ḥadīth* and the opinions of the Companions of the Prophet.

Quranic Evidence. Wilful murder is certainly a much more serious offence than theft. The Qur'ān ordains death sentence for this offence. But it provides as well that if the heirs of the deceased agree, the accused may be saved from death, on payment of blood-money. There is no reason, therefore, that this proviso should not be applicable to cases of theft as well. As a matter of fact, the majority of our jurists say that if the owner of the stolen property wants compensation for his loss, the hand of the thief shall not be cut. And if he wants that the hand be cut off, he shall not be entitled to compensation (*Muḥīṭ*).

Again, the offences of waging war against the State and highway robbery and dacoity with or without murder are undoubtedly the most atrocious crimes imaginable. For these offences the Qur'ān provides the following sentence : "They should be killed or crucified, or their hands and feet should be cut off on opposite sides or they should be imprisoned" (v. 33). Now, if these offences can be punished with imprisonment, why theft cannot be? To understand one Quranic verse it is always necessary to keep in view all the other verses on the subject.

Ḥadīth Evidence. If amputation were the only sentence for all cases of theft, the Prophet could not possibly have said that there shall be no cutting off of the hands for the theft of property worth less than a certain amount, or the theft of this or that article or the theft from this or that place. The *aḥādīth* go a long way to show that the Prophet considered amputation the maximum and not the only punishment for theft. Some of these traditions show that in certain cases even nominal sentence can meet the ends of justice.

'Umar's Opinion. 'Umar, known to be the most strict administrator of Islam, is reported to have said that there shall be no cutting off of the hand during a famine.

Jurists' Efforts to Make Amputation Impossible. All this evidence proves beyond doubt that the punishment for theft and for other offences given in the Qur'ān is the maximum punishment that can be awarded and not the only punishment for the offence. But, unfortunately, our jurists have failed to appreciate the point, with the result that, as in the case of adultery, so in the case of theft, they have, in some cases for illogical reasons, framed the law relating to theft in a way that the sentence of amputation becomes impossible.

An Interesting Point Raised by Rāzī. Imām Fakhr al-Dīn Rāzī, in his great commentary, *Tafsīr-i Kabīr*, has raised a very interesting point regarding the Quranic verse about theft. He says:

" This verse [Q. v. 38] is open to different interpretations for the following reasons :

"(*a*) Amputation could not be the punishment for every theft, and the verse has not fixed the amount of stolen property for which the hand of the thief would be cut off.

"(*b*) The word *Yad*, i.e., 'hand,' can be used for fingers only. For an example, if I say on oath that I shall not touch a certain person with my hand, and then I touch him with my finger, I shall be liable to pay *Kaffārah* for breaking the oath. Thus the word 'hand' has been used here for a finger. This word can as well be used for palm up to wrist, and for the forearm up to elbow. The verse does not say how much of the hand is to be cut off.

"(*c*) The verse does not say whether the right or the left hand or both the hands have to be amputated.

"Therefore the way for *Ijtihād*, i.e. interpretation according to one's own lights, on all these details is left open."

Rāzī's question, what is hand, is really an important question. As a matter of fact, there has been a difference of opinion as to what part of the hand is to be cut off. The majority of jurists say that the hand is to be cut off at the wrist. But there are some who say that the whole of the arm up to the armpit is to be cut off, and there are some though very few who say that it suffices to cut off the fingers only.

Qaṭa'. The word *qaṭa*' means "to cut". This word and the word *yad*, i.e. "hand" have been used together at another place in the Qur'ān, as well :

فَلَمَّا رَأَيْنَهُ أَكْبَرْنَهُ وَقَطَّعْنَ أَيْدِيَهُنَّ

["When these women saw him, they deemed him great, and cut their hands (in amazement)" (xii. 31).]

Here *Qaṭa*' means to cut and injure and not to cut off. Is it not possible to give the same meaning to this word in the verse relating to theft? If it is possible, it would be sufficient to cut the hand of the thief in a way to make it totally or partially useless.

Forgiveness. The Qur'ān provides for pardon in cases of theft as well. But, for reasons best known to them, the majority of our jurists say that theft cannot be forgiven. The *Tafsīr-i Kabīr* says:

"The words of the verse [Q. v. 39] show that if the thief repents, God would accept his repentance. If it be said that the verse mentions reform with repentance and therefore only repentance is not sufficient, I will say that repentance with reform means a sincere repentance with a resolve to behave better in future. The question arises whether a person who shows repentance before the sentence is executed would escape amputation. Some men of learning among the *Tābi'īn* (successors to the Companions) are of opinion that the man would be saved from punishment. This is according to the plain meaning of the verse. But the majority of the jurists say that the sentence shall be executed even after repentance."

Section 562 of the Pakistan Criminal Procedure Code practically means the same thing, although its application is much more limited.

Amputation in Serious Cases of Theft. We do, occasionally, come across some very dark and serious cases of theft. We know, as well, that there are some people who are hardened and habitual thieves. Cutting off a hand in such cases would not be a harsh punishment at all.

Finis